Atomic Accomplice

How Canada deals in deadly deceit

by Paul McKay

Foreword by David Suzuki

Printed on *Envirographic 100* -
100% post-consumer recycled paper.
100% processed chlorine free and acid free.

ACKNOWLEDGEMENTS

I would like to thank the following for their advice and assistance:

David Suzuki, Peter Prebble, Morag Carter, Stan Segel, Maxine Ruvinksy,
Paul Gervan, Kathy Daw, Bilbo Poynter, Doug and Susan Gander, Clifford
Maynes, David Martin, Gordon Edwards, Jamie Swift,
Ralph Torrie, Doug Banwell.
Any errors or omissions are entirely my own.

For more journalism and jazz compositions
www.paulmckay.com

For more about Fabio Rosa's Solar Foundation
www.ideaas.org.br

For more about The David Suzuki Foundation
www.davidsuzuki.org

ABOUT THE AUTHOR

Paul McKay has won Canada's top journalism awards for investigative,
magazine and business writing. He is also a past winner of the Atkinson
Fellowship in Public Policy, and past Pierre Berton writer-in-residence. He
has written for the Ottawa Citizen, Toronto Star, Globe and Mail,
Harrowsmith, Maclean's, and CBC television and radio documentaries,
and is on the advisory board of the
Canadian Centre for Investigative Reporting.

OTHER BOOKS BY PAUL MCKAY

Electric Empire: The Inside Story of Ontario Hydro
The Pilgrim and the Cowboy
The Roman Empire: The Unauthorized Life
and Times of Stephen Roman
Inspired Alchemy: The Ecology of Genius and Joy

"I will write peace on your wings and you will fly all over the world.

Sadako Sasaki

Inspired by an ancient Japanese legend which promised good luck
to those who make 1,000 paper cranes, 12-year old Hiroshima bomb victim
Sadako Sasaki made 644 *orizuro* before leukaemia claimed her in 1955.
Her classmates completed her mission, and Sadako was buried
with 1,000 paper cranes. In 1958, a statue in her honour was built
at the Hiroshima Peace Park, and since then millions have been inspired
to make paper peace cranes.

To hear "*Song for Sadako*" go to:
www.paulmckay.com

Dedicated
to:

June Callwood,
who inspired others to comfort the afflicted
and afflict the comfortable
&
Neil Reynolds,
who emboldened others to report
the news without fear or favour.

Cover design: Summit Sound
Photographs by Paul McKay or in Public Domain.

ISBN-978-0-9813380-0-2   333-72

www.paulmckay.com

CONTENTS

Foreword by David Suzuki

Preface
Introduction

In August, 1945 the civilian cities of Hiroshima and Nagasaki were destroyed by the "Fat Man" and "Little Boy" atomic bombs, which fissioned masses of enriched uranium and plutonium equal to the lead inside a single shotgun shell.

Robert Oppenheimer (l) was the Manhattan Project chief atomic bomb designer, and Gen. Leslie Groves (r) commanded the U.S. bomb production effort. They later clashed over developing the hydrogen bomb (below), which has one thousand times more explosive power.

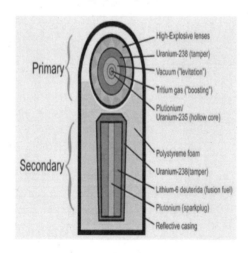

Canada's unique Chalk River heavy-water reactor was originally built to produce plutonium for U.S. bombs. Replicas for military use were later built in the U.S., Russia, Britain, France, China, Israel, India, Pakistan and Iran.

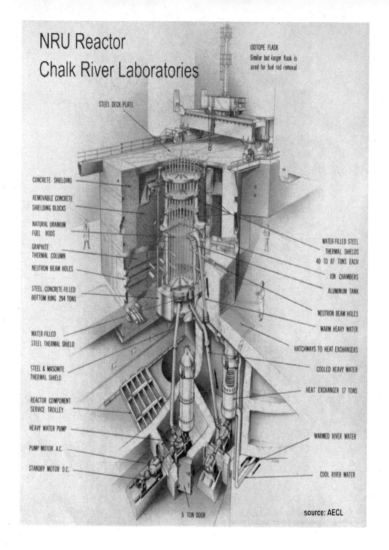

NRU Reactor
Chalk River Laboratories

ISOTOPE FLASK
Similar but larger flask is
used for fuel rod removal

STEEL DECK PLATE

CONCRETE SHIELDING

REMOVABLE CONCRETE
SHIELDING BLOCKS

NATURAL URANIUM
FUEL RODS

GRAPHITE
THERMAL COLUMN

NEUTRON BEAM HOLES

STEEL, CONCRETE-FILLED
BOTTOM RING 294 TONS

WATER-FILLED
STEEL THERMAL SHIELD

STEEL & MASONITE
THERMAL SHIELD

REACTOR COMPONENT
SERVICE TROLLEY

HEAVY WATER PUMP

PUMP MOTOR A.C.

STANDBY MOTOR D.C.

WATER-FILLED STEEL
THERMAL SHIELDS
40 TO 87 TONS EACH

ION CHAMBERS

ALUMINUM TANK

NEUTRON BEAM HOLES

WARM HEAVY WATER

HATCHWAYS TO HEAT EXCHANGERS

COOLED HEAVY WATER

HEAT EXCHANGER 17 TONS

WARMED RIVER WATER

COOL RIVER WATER

5 TON DOOR

source: AECL

Due to its military genesis, later generation CANDU power reactors produce higher volumes of plutonium than other commercial reactors. Another feature allows constant re-fuelling, which can maximize plutonium production and mask clandestine bomb efforts.

The Cold War began when Russian cipher clerk Igor Gouzenko defected in Ottawa. De-coded documents showed Josef Stalin and his secret police chief Lavrentii Beria had an atomic espionage ring operating in war-time Canada, Britain and the U.S.

Indira Gandhi approved using a Canadian reactor to make plutonium for India's "Smiling Buddha" bomb test in 1974 (blast site shown above). Pakistan's Ali Bhutto sought a CANDU to make a rival "Sword of Islam", which detonated in 1998.

All Canadian prime ministers, including four generations of Liberal leaders, have since 1945 vowed to pursue atomic arms control, while promoting "Team Canada" sales of CANDU reactors and uranium. Recipients included several dictators, and Li Peng, China's infamous 'Butcher of Beijing'.

David Suzuki makes a passionate case for green power at a 'switch on' ceremony in Kingston, Canada.

Brazilian green engineer Fabio Rosa delivers safe, low-cost solar-electric power to villages in South America, Africa and Asia. His IDEAAS Foundation leases household systems which provide lights, water pumping and power for small tools for $15 per month.

FOREWORD

As a scientist, I consider the release of energy by splitting atoms to be one of humanity's great intellectual milestones. The purest of all sciences - theoretical physics – is meant to demonstrate the enormous potential of applying scientific insights for human use. But just as Pandora's curiosity led her to open a jar and release the forces of evil, scientists too have pried open nature's deepest secrets to liberate elements of vast destructive potential.

A renowned military hero, General Dwight D. Eisenhower, introduced the concept of "atoms for peace" in 1953. It was an appealing notion to "turn swords into plowshares", but like the current oxymoron of "clean coal" his metaphor hid a darker reality.

One of the Canadian legacies of the World War Two rush to create the first atomic bomb was an outstanding group of physicists, many of whom remained in Canada at war's end. They turned their expertise into another enterprise, harnessing the atom in a Canadian technology, the CANDU reactor.

Canadians think of ourselves as global good guys. After all, one of our Prime Ministers, Lester Pearson, won a Nobel Peace Prize. And we have watched with pride as our soldiers, wearing the powder blue helmets of the United Nations, served as global peacekeepers. The CANDU apparently fit this image, by using the atom to generate electricity while also offering international sales benefits for Canada.

But a Canadian reactor, purportedly donated for research in India, provided the fuel for a bomb that was exploded in 1974. This revealed the terrible truth about nuclear energy. The twin potentials – weapons and reactors – are conjoined. No amount of monitoring and inspection can control the fate of radioisotopes, nor prevent the construction of bombs. In a time of increasing concern about climate change, nuclear reactors are being touted as a source of green energy. But this meticulously researched book makes it clear there is no way to separate fuel for nuclear reactors from fuel for atomic weapons.

This is why non-proliferation treaties and international inspection agencies are failing to prevent the increase in nations with nuclear arms, many using Canadian uranium and Canadian nuclear technology. And, despite all the promise, nuclear power has turned out to be frightfully expensive and unreliable, with a still unresolved problem of what to do with highly toxic radioactive waste with a half-life of tens of thousands of years.

The conjunction of multiple issues – economic meltdown, climate change, peak oil, escalating energy demand, health issues – has created a huge crisis. *But this can also be an opportunity to look at the entire picture and get it right.* Fossil and nuclear fuels are finite, not limitless. So any truly sustainable energy future must be based on renewable resources. Furthermore, burning fossil and nuclear fuels creates greenhouse gases or radioactive wastes. And the fact that there is a direct link between nuclear plants and the fuel for the creation of nuclear bombs makes the spectre of terrorists or rogue countries all the more real.

Paul McKay's "*Atomic Accomplice*" provides the history, science, and economic background of the purveyors of nuclear fuel and reactors, and outlines global future energy options to wean ourselves from non-renewable sources. In the end, he is correct in pointing out that only one nuclear furnace - our Sun - is an energy source that is effectively endless, and can promote both peace and prosperity.

David T. Suzuki, scientist and broadcaster

When you complete Paul McKay's book, it will be clear why the *Bulletin of the Atomic Scientist* clock is set at five minutes to midnight. Far from the Canadian image of our country as a "boy scout" nation working to promote a more peaceful world, McKay uncovers a side of Canadian public policy driven by greed, secrecy, deceit and a willingness to put global safety at risk for the sake of commercial opportunity. Much of that proliferation peril stems from Saskatchewan uranium exports.

Atomic Accomplice does not stop here, however. The last chapters of his book open a fascinating discussion on how Canadians can help unravel the atomic weapons proliferation mess our country has been such a large part of creating. McKay offers policy suggestions aimed not only at reducing the weapons proliferation risk, but at simultaneously addressing the climate crisis and the need for a safe, renewable energy future. *Atomic Accomplice* will be of interest to both the lay reader and to those in academic and policy making circles. It is a must read for all who want to use an understanding of our history to build a more just, peaceful and sustainable world.

Peter Prebble,
Saskatchewan Environmental Society

PREFACE

"I ask you to stop and think for a moment what it would mean to have nuclear weapons in so many hands, in hands of countries large and small, stable and unstable, responsible and irresponsible, scattered throughout the world. There would be no rest for anyone then, no stability, no real security, and no chance of effective disarmament."

John F. Kennedy, 1963

"*Follow the money*" is an axiom at the heart of investigative journalism.

In the early 20th Century, intrepid reporters like Lincoln Steffens, Ida Tarbell, and Charles Russell used the technique to trace bribes paid to U.S. Congress members, expose the secret financial reach of monopolies like Standard Oil, or reveal that blocks of sickness-infested slum tenements in New York City were owned by the wealthiest church in America.

Later, Woodward and Bernstein cracked the Watergate case by tracing the flow of funds in President Richard Nixon's secret re-election slush fund. More recently in Canada, a tenacious team at the CBC's *Fifth Estate* spent two decades exhuming payments made in the Mulroney-Airbus affair, and *Globe and Mail* reporter Daniel Leblanc bared the flow of hidden political patronage dollars embedded in the Chretien-era sponsorship scandal.

The venerable "follow the money" technique works because it relies heavily on forensic facts - documents, deeds and dollars paid or received - rather than what those involved claim or deny. It is thus the toughest abrasive for scouring out lies, evasions, spin or propaganda.

This book follows the *atoms*. Or more precisely, it audits the trail of Canadian fissile elements, sensitive materials, reactor sales, and laboratory secrets which have abetted the global proliferation of atomic and hydrogen bombs.

Canada has been dealing atoms since 1942, when the Mackenize King war cabinet approved joining the Allied nuclear bomb effort known as the Manhattan Project. It supplied key ingredients to U.S. production plants and weapons laboratories making the weapons that destroyed Hiroshima and Nagasaki.

15

The prevailing myth is that this tragedy ended Canada's involvement with the military atom. But that is false. Spanning six decades and more than a dozen countries, this investigation confirms that - like a radioactive plume spreading out concentrically from an atomic blast - Canada has accelerated the global dispersal of weapons-related elements, technologies, and secrets.

Much of this happened below the public and political radar, and has already helped in the making of nuclear bombs currently stored in the arsenals of the U.S., Britain, Russia, France, Israel, India, and Pakistan. Canada has also dealt atomic supplies and secrets to military dictatorships in Argentina, Taiwan, Romania, South Korea and Communist China.

We are still engaged in this deadly diaspora. Canada currently exports 7.3 million kilograms of uranium annually.[1] When fissioned in any reactor of any owner or origin, this will create some 19,000 kilograms of plutonium each year, or enough to make 2,300 warheads annually if it is extracted from the spent fuel.[2] These annual uranium exports also contain 52,000 kilograms of fissile uranium-235, or enough to make 2,600 atomic bombs each year.[3]

Because it is essentially immortal, this 'embedded' Canadian plutonium and U_{235} will imperil global security for millennia because it will outlast hundreds of future governments in the recipient countries. Or, for all intents and purposes, the rest of human history.

This is not merely my view, or my conjecture. It is not hyperbole. It is a stark, fundamental fact of physics which no honest scientist can deny. The fission of uranium and the creation of plutonium are inextricably entwined like fire and smoke, or the twisted double helix of DNA.

For this reason, physicists aptly named plutonium after the deathless and diabolical Greek god of the underworld. Standing outside nature itself, it embeds a dimension of destruction almost beyond imagining. A fissioned mass the size of a stick of chewing gum can destroy a city.

---

[1] World Nuclear Association. Canadian uranium exports in 2008 were 7,330 tonnes.
[2] Plutonium production from a CANDU reactor averages 2.6 grams per kilogram of spent fuel. Calculation: 7.3 million kilograms (7,330 tonnes) x .0026 (ratio of plutonium per tonne of uranium) divided by 8 (kilograms required per bomb).
[3] Fissile uranium-235 content is calculated as 7.3 million kilograms x .0072 (ratio of U_{235} in natural uranium) divided by 20 (kilograms required per bomb).

16

Canada leads the world in uranium exports. Ergo, it leads the world in collateral plutonium proliferation, and the spread of fissile U_{235}. This earns more than $1 billion in current cash flow, but uranium's alter ego will court calamity for centuries to come because embedded in these exports is enough fissile material to make almost 5,000 warheads each year.

This trade fits the profile of a psychopath, or black marketeer. It will be a tough truth for Canadians to swallow. We pride ourselves on our standing as an 'honest broker' in international relations, and for the peace-keeping forces we have sent, often at great cost in lives lost, to far-off places where civilians are at the mercy of murderous conflicts.

But 'following the atoms' proves that we are a boy-scout nation with a very dirty secret. It has been under-written by $30 billion in taxpayer dollars, greased with secret bribes to win export deals, and buried in decades of deceit by official Ottawa.[4]

My job as a journalist is to exhume the true facts. My obligation as a world citizen is to alert my fellow Canadians when those facts prove that this sinister trade secret continues to imperil other people and the planet. I hope readers find I have done both honestly. And that the facts which follow will compel them to act.

---

[4] Kory Teneyeke, chief of communications for Prime Minister Stephen Harper, told the Canadian Press in June, 2009 that "The government has put $30 billion into AECL over its history, and it's been one of the largest sinkholes of government money in the history of Canada". See also: "Federal Government Subsidies to AECL", Tom Adams, 2006; "The Dismal Economics of Candu", George Lerner, Policy Options, 1996; "Fifty Years of Futile Funding"; Dave Martin/Campaign for Nuclear Phaseout, 2003

INTRODUCTION

"The unleashed atom has changed everything save our modes of thinking, and thus we drift towards unparalleled catastrophe."

Albert Einstein

"When you see something that is technically sweet, you go ahead and you argue about what to do with it only after you have had your technical success. That is the way it was with the atom bomb."

J. Robert Oppenheimer

$E = mc^2$.

Everyone recognises Albert Einstein's famed blackboard-and-chalk formula. Prophetic and revelatory, it unveiled the laws which bind the invisible, sub-atomic architecture of our universe. Perhaps the most elegant equation in physics, it also triggered the Faustian insight into how to break one of those laws - the 'curve of binding energy' - which keeps atoms from splitting.

When that secret was first rent in 1945, the human species invented an atomic means to destroy itself, much of animate life, even the cloth of Creation itself.

Witnessing the first bomb test in the New Mexico desert, physicist J. Robert Oppenheimer murmured a fragment of ancient Asian scripture: 'Now I am become Death, Shatterer of Worlds." His aide, a military munitions expert who had wired the bomb detonators, had a more profane assessment: "Now we are all sons of bitches."

Plutonium = forever.

Far fewer might remember this epigram, sometimes silk-screened onto placards of peace protesters lamenting the escalating atomic arms race during the Cold War era, when global arsenals peaked at 65,000 warheads. It's a safe bet most did not own a degree in physics. Yet their equation was equally lucid, and accurate.

18

Once created, plutonium is essentially immortal.[5] Forged from uranium inside the crucible of an atomic reactor, the laws of physics dictate that it will remain latently lethal for hundreds of centuries. Plutonium can be transmuted or 'burned up' in only two ways: in the instant an atomic bomb detonates, or by the slower, contained neutron bombardment inside an atomic reactor. But this benefit is illusory, because the latter reaction requires using more uranium, which in turn breeds more plutonium.

Only a plum-sized sphere of plutonium is needed to make an atomic weapon which can be delivered by inter-continental bomber, submarine-launched missile, Piper Cub airplane, or suicide bomber with a brief-case or backpack.

Six decades ago, Einstein's fateful equation - and his own ominous 1939 warning about Nazi atomic research to U.S. President Franklin Roosevelt - underpinned an effort by Allied scientists to create humanity's first atomic bombs. In August, 1945, this vapourized two civilian targets in Japan. That in turn triggered an atomic arms race among an ever-growing list of nations in a 'nuclear-armed crowd'. The latest entrants are North Korea and Iran.

The Hiroshima bomb used the atomic element U_{235}. It instantly killed 140,000, injured another 70,000, and destroyed ninety-per cent of all buildings.[6] The Nagasaki bomb used Pu_{239}, derived from uranium. It killed 70,000 [7] and injured 25,000.

In the following decade, the first American and Soviet hydrogen 'superbombs' would combine both, plus the man-made isotopes deuterium (heavy water) and tritium. Up to one thousand times more powerful than mere A-bombs, the first H-bombs would make even their inventors shudder with pride, fear and shame.

Uranium. Plutonium. Deuterium. Tritium. One could call them the four horsemen of an atomic apocalypse. At the dawn of the 21st century, some 27,000 nuclear warheads are still aimed at human populations.[8] No place on

---

[5] Plutonium 239, a human-made fissile element, has a radioactive decay rate, or half-life, of 24,300 years. This means it gradually loses its mass through the emission or loss of alpha energy or particles. A kilogram of plutonium will be reduced to one half kilogram after 243 centuries.
[6] "Nuclear Weapons: Report of the Secretary General"; United Nations; 1980
[7] Based on estimates submitted to the United Nations, including deaths from radiation and blast effects as of December, 1945.
[8] "Bomb Scare"; Cirincione; pg xiii

19

Earth is safe from them. No country, citizen or species is out of range, or exempt from the corona of terror they embody.

This is the story of how one 'boy scout' nation helped make this happen - and continues to be an atomic accomplice.

Canada, of course, has never produced an atomic or hydrogen bomb. Soon after the shattering blasts at Hiroshima and Nagasaki, and despite the technical ability to do so, Ottawa formally resolved to never make them. It has kept this vow for six decades, and so earned considerable ethical prestige in global nuclear non-proliferation affairs.

But, in truth, Canada's nuclear record is far from innocent. Our nation produced research and materials for the first atomic bombs. Many of the émigré scientists who worked in the Montreal contingent of the U.S.-led Manhattan Project later dispersed to Russia, Britain, and France - where their secrets were unveiled to abet rival weapons programs.

Later, Canada was the prime supplier of uranium for the Cold War atomic arsenals of America and Britain. It was exported, then enriched into bomb-grade uranium, or converted to plutonium, for warheads. While promising to support non-proliferation treaties, Canada supplied nuclear 'gunpowder' to our allies so that they could build and aim warheads at Cold War enemies.

No surprise - that provoked Russia (and later Communist China) into making ever more atomic weapons with ever increasing explosive power and deliverable accuracy. To counter that threat and obtain the maximum bang for the buck, the U.S. and Britain ordered still more, and more efficient, nuclear weapons of mass destruction. That required Canadian uranium.

Ottawa was more than pleased to sell. So military uranium sales soared, as did Ottawa's diplomatic duplicities when international nuclear non-proliferation talks and treaties began threatening Canada's uranium sales. And Ottawa's own balance sheet. At the time, every ounce of exported uranium was profitably brokered by a federal crown company, Eldorado Nuclear.

By 1965, the U.S. and Britain had amassed some 20,000 nuclear bombs made principally with Canadian uranium - an 'overkill' level so obvious that even their generals agreed recycling could keep those arsenals intact. An end to military uranium purchases was announced. Ottawa was devastated:

20

Canada was the world's largest producer. With virtually no customers, mining companies would crash. Thousands of miners would be thrown out of work. Ghost towns would appear.

No one knew this better than Nobel Peace laureate and Liberal Prime Minister Lester Pearson. His Ontario electoral riding included Elliot Lake, and the largest, richest, most profitable uranium mines then in the world.

Pearson's adroit response was to have the Canadian government *itself* buy prodigious amounts of uranium for a fixed price. This saved the biggest and best-connected companies, but predictably left a federal Crown corporation called Uranium Canada with a huge inventory and virtually no buyers.

To solve that dilemma, Pearson's successor, Pierre Trudeau, endorsed a secret, illegal cartel designed to drive up the world price, sell the stockpiled uranium at a profit, and put the surviving Canadian uranium companies back in the black. To keep this cartel hidden, Trudeau's cabinet approved a federal regulation forbidding any public disclosure - including by Canadian journalists or media outlets - under penalty of heavy fines and imprisonment.

By the time this cartel was exposed (initially in Australia, a cartel member), Ottawa was spearheading a new strategy: it would prevent the international spread of 'military' atoms by dispersing 'peaceful' CANDU reactors and uranium to all corners of the globe.

Henceforth, Canadian uranium would only be exported and sold for use in civilian power reactors. The same terms would apply to global sales of CANDU reactors. In an ingenious example of 'tied selling', both would be offered as a long-term package, be subject to safeguards meant to prevent diversion into military uses, and come with alluring loans and payment terms.

This would allow Canada to salvage a crippled domestic uranium industry, globally market its nascent CANDU reactor technology, win plaudits from developing countries, and take the high diplomatic road in international talks aimed at curbing nuclear weapons proliferation. Nothing, it seemed, could prevent Canada from re-claiming its boy-scout honour, while racking up impressive 'atoms for peace' sales of reactors and uranium.

Then in May, 1974, India detonated its first atomic bomb. With macabre triumph, its inventors officially hailed it as their "Smiling Buddha". It was triggered by plutonium created in the Canadian-supplied reactor. Later, a carbon copy built by Indian scientists would be used to create plutonium and tritium for India's hydrogen bombs.

The Indian claim that it had made merely a 'peaceful nuclear device' - and not an atomic bomb - fooled no one. In Ottawa, a furious Prime Minister Trudeau privately ripped into the nuclear mandarins who had blithely assured him this could not happen. Publicly, he announced that India was immediately cut off from all further nuclear assistance.

But more than one atomic genie was already out of the bottle. Canada had also supplied India's regional arch-rival, Pakistan, with a larger version of the 'peaceful' reactor. Within hours of the Indian blast, the Islamic Prime Minister Ali Bhutto publicly vowed Pakistan would reach nuclear parity. To wild cheers on the streets of Karachi, the 'Sword of Islam' was detonated in 1998, in part with the help of the Canada. Once again, far too late, Ottawa put a country on its atomic pariah list.

But in the meantime, Canada had sold another to the military government in Taiwan, and scaled-up versions of the same reactor (configured to produce electricity) to military dictatorships in Argentina, Romania, South Korea, and Communist China.

The Indian explosion in 1974, using plutonium created in a Canadian-designed and supplied reactor, offered public proof that the only dividing line between the 'peaceful' and 'military' atom was *intent*. The same reactor could be used to produce power, or plutonium. In fact, an inherent feature is that it produces both, simultaneously.

The Indian and Pakistani blasts also confirmed that policing atomic intent is virtually impossible. The Canadian reactors were supplied only after solemn, written promises were made that the nuclear technology would be used for exclusively peaceful purposes. Once the reactors were delivered and operational, both countries resolutely lied to Ottawa about the covert plutonium use until after their first bomb had been detonated.

Some observers, particularly Canadians implicated at the supplier end, cast this as a hardluck case of 'boy scout' betrayed. Twice.

But the truth is that Canada's atomic insiders have known, since the Manhattan Project, that the CANDU prototype *was conceived as a military plutonium production reactor*. At the time, Allied scientists were racing to discover whether U_{235}, or Pu_{239}, was the best route to the first atomic bomb.

22

It took $2 billion ($24 billion in current dollars), and the single most concerted scientific effort in history, to discover that both would work.

Canada's primary role was to supply natural uranium, from which fissile U_{235} atoms were gleaned at a vast enrichment complex in the U.S. But the Montreal group was also charged with discovering the best way of producing plutonium for future Allied *arsenals*. Because the amalgam of British, French and Canadian scientists had access to the world's first stock of deuterium, they devised the first reactor which created plutonium after natural uranium was bombarded with neutrons travelling through a deuterium (heavy water) filled tank.

This military genesis explains why the CANDU reactor typically produces 2.6 grams of plutonium per kilogram of used uranium fuel - the highest ratio among all commercial reactor designs. In the process, it also creates a steady supply of the bomb ingredient, tritium.

Uranium. Plutonium. Deuterium. Tritium. All were used or produced in the post-war reactor built in Chalk River, Ontario. Its' plutonium was shipped to the U.S. military for bomb production, until the U.S. built replicas of its own in South Carolina. And the émigré scientists who co-designed the CANDU prototype (and learned how to separate plutonium from intensely radioactive used fuel) later passed on these secrets to atomic bomb makers in Britain, France, Russia, China, and eventually Israel (via France).

Extensive evidence of this will be seen in later chapters. For now, the point is that the unique CANDU reactor is essentially a plutonium factory scaled up and fitted with boilers to produce electricity. For an electric utility interested only in peaceful uses, it is a power reactor which incidentally includes plutonium and tritium.

However, as India and Pakistan have shown, for a nation determined to acquire bomb-grade plutonium (or tritium for H-bombs) under the cover of a civilian reactor producing electric power, the CANDU has no rival. With its diplomatically unassailable (and unpoliceable) veil of innocence, it produces electric power, plutonium and tritium.

For dictators and despots, this disguise is its best virtue: it is the perfect way to keep intent secret until it is too late. The CANDU comes with its own shield of diplomatic immunity - even from the country which supplies it, Canada. And there is no doubt weapons can be made from 'reactor-grade' plutonium. The U.S. first tested just such a bomb, made from civilian reactor spent fuel, at its Nevada test site in 1962.[9]

But the proliferation risk is not confined to which governments are current or past Canadian reactor and uranium customers. Even if both are initially used only for peaceful purposes, the used fuel will always, inevitably contain plutonium. And because it is effectively indestructible and immortal, these exports amount to a gamble that nothing sinister will happen to that plutonium for millenia.

Yet the very nature of plutonium - its effectively ageless decay rate, and its intrinsic capacity for destruction - defies every assurance that peaceful atoms cannot one day be converted into military ones. Every time uranium is fissioned in a reactor, plutonium is created.[10]

Canada is the world's largest producer and exporter of uranium. Mines in northern Saskatchewan are among the largest and richest ever discovered. With the world price spiking, more are slated to open - even in the pristine heart of arctic Nunavut. There, the French state company Areva plans to operate five uranium mines producing up to 4,000 tonnes of processed ore per year for seventeen years. Once burned in a reactor, this cumulative 68,000 tonnes of exported uranium will transmute into enough plutonium for 22,000 atomic bombs.[11]

Canada has already sold CANDU reactors abroad, and is gearing up to sell more. All of this atomic commerce is being consecrated by official Ottawa promises that Canada's nuclear exports will be for peaceful purposes only.

Atomic Accomplice shows that this is not a mere mistaken belief, or even the diplomatic equivalent of Canadian trade and proliferation policy being made on a wing and a prayer. It is a deliberate, dangerous deception. The half-life of plutonium, and its latent lethality, defy all such assurances.

---

[9] "Additional Information Regarding Underground Nuclear Weapon Test of Reactor Grade Material"; U.S. Department of Energy

[10] A more exact description is that U_{238} is transmuted into Pu_{239}.

[11] Calculation: 4,000 tonnes x 17 years x 1,000 (kilograms) divided by 2.6 (kilograms of Pu_{239} per tonne of uranium) divided by 8 kilograms per weapon.

In one of human history's great irony's, the latent peril embedded in the Atomic Age was inaugurated by the elegant mathematics of Einstein, and two scientific peers inspired to verify his famous $E = mc^2$ equation at the more prosaic level of laboratory physics.

In February, 1932 the British journal *Nature* published a letter by the esteemed Cambridge University physicist James Chadwick which unveiled the existence of a sub-atomic particle called the neutron. More importantly, his experiment showed that by 'aiming' neutrons emanating from radioactive sources at non-radioactive elements, those targeted atoms could be transmuted and produce astonishing bursts of energy.[12]

The letter caused a sensation in the world of physics, and ignited a competitive academic quest to replicate Chadwick's discovery of the neutron. In April, 1932, *Nature* published a summary by a second Cambridge physics team, led by John D. Cockcroft, which used the same technique to target and alter different atoms.[13]

Taken together, the Cambridge experiments verified the existence of the neutron, its powerful capacity to transmute other elements, and Einstein's famous formula. The discovery was Promethean. We could now peer deep inside the sub-atomic structure of the universe - and alter it.

It did not take long for other physicists to discern that this could also alter the fate of humankind. The neutron, they knew, might eventually produce prodigious amounts of energy which could be harnessed to fuel atomic power plants - or forge fission bombs of unimaginable destruction.[14] For the next six years, experimental physicists in universities and laboratories around the globe raced to replicate and augment the Cambridge discovery,

---

[12] Technically, these experiments proved a phenomena known as neutron absorption, not atom splitting.

[13] In this experiment, the bombarded element was lithium. The 1932 Cockcroft experiment was entirely benign in intent, but two decades later lithium would prove to be a critical ingredient in hydrogen bombs.

[14] The Hungarian physicist Leo Szilard is widely acknowledged to have first discerned the physics potential of a fission bomb, and with alerting Einstein and Churchill to the prospect of Nazi Germany acquiring it first. After Hiroshima, Szilard led a doomed campaign by scientists to prevent atomic proliferation.

using different, neutron-rich radioactive sources and aiming them at different elements.[15]

The challenge now was to *control* the phenomena. That would require finding elements which emanated a steady, reliable stream of neutrons, and targets which consistently produced even more neutrons when they were deliberately hit. Then multiple fissions could happen in a continuous sequence. This could occur within millionths of a second, but only within a confined space - akin to trapping lightening in a bottle.

Complex calculations made in England, Germany, Denmark, Italy, France, Russia, Japan, and the United States hinted that this chain reaction was theoretically possible. Tantalized, intellectually enchanted, and driven by a competitive quest to make their mark, some of the brightest minds of the time bent to solve the secret. Remarkably, in a pre-war fraternal spirit of 'open source' science, they readily shared their results with each other.

By late 1938 the most promising candidates had been narrowed down to 'unstable' naturally-occurring elements at the bottom of the periodic table, like uranium and radium. Not unlike prize-fighters shedding weight before a championship bout, these occupied a special class of elements because they had a mass so dense they occasionally discarded neutrons to achieve atomic stability and structural strength.

Inevitably, scientists intuited that putting two comparably powerful but unstable atomic 'prize-fighters' inside the same experimental ring would produce the fastest, most furious flurry of neutrons.

Fatefully, this happened in Nazi Germany one month after the chilling *Kristalnacht* anti-Jewish SS rampage in November, 1938, and mere months before Hitler's armies would invade Poland. Relying on key prior experiments by Enrico Fermi in Rome, and the famous Frederic Joliot-Curie team in Paris, German physicists[16] proved that aiming a weak neutron stream at uranium split those atoms and unleashed an even stronger surge of neutrons.

The net gain in neutrons was barely calculable, given the tiny size of the irradiated uranium target. But it was like depositing one dollar in a bank

---

[15] Perhaps the most notable was that of Italy's Enrico Fermi and his protégé Bruno Pontecorvo. Fermi later achieved history's first sustained atomic chain reaction. Pontecorvo achieved fame in the fields of cosmic ray and neutrino physics, but also infamy for defecting to Stalin's Russia with atom bomb secrets.
[16] Hahn, Meitner, Strassman

26

which instantly generated 120 pennies, which then exponentially generated more and more pennies. The bigger the uranium 'deposit', the bigger and faster compound neutron interest would occur. If enough uranium were compressed into an enclosed space, then bombarded with neutrons, the runaway chain reaction would be explosive.

Facing Nazi persecution, one member of the German team, Lise Meitner, had sought safe haven in Stockholm. It was she and her nephew, Otto Frisch, who intuited the secret of the nuclear chain reaction.[17] This was conveyed to the Nobel Prize-winning Danish physicist, Niels Bohr. He instantly grasped the military meaning of the experiment. Despite some apprehension, Bohr publicly announced the discovery soon after and the two Germans detailed their proof in the February, 1939 edition of *Nature*.

Now the fateful secret was out. Ears immediately pricked up in Nazi Berlin, at Britain's leading research centres, at an advanced physics lab in Berkeley, California, and in the intelligence antennae of Josef Stalin's notorious chief of secret police, Laventrii Beria. Soon each country would be pursuing fission bombs in deadly earnest, and Canada would be drawn into the drama.

By the time Hitler's panzer divisions launched their surprise attack into Poland in September, 1939, the key ingredient for making atomic weapons had been gleaned. It was natural uranium, which actually comprises two isotopes of slightly different atomic weight.

Physicists quickly discovered that the ratio of U_{238} isotopes to U_{235} was 140:1.[18] This fact had enormous consequences, because only the extremely rare U_{235} isotopes emanated their own neutrons, or was fissile. This explained why ordinary uranium emitted only weak radioactive energy, and why atomic explosions could not occur naturally.

But the physicists also discovered that by aiming neutrons at the plentiful non-fissile U_{238} isotopes an entirely new fissile isotope - plutonium - could

---

[17] Despite her brilliance, Meitner was cheated of the credit for this discovery because she was an Austrian born Jew. Under Nazi laws, her name could not be attached to the German scientific paper which announced the discovery, and the Nobel Prize was awarded solely to Hahn.
[18] Cited in "Canada's Nuclear Story"; Wilfred Eggleston, page 14

be created.[19] Like U_{235}, the fissile nature of Pu_{239} meant physicists could aim neutrons at it and create bursts of atomic power by breaking the force known as the curve of binding energy.

But there was yet another maddening paradox: a trade-off between accuracy and timing.

While the U_{235} isotopes could be hit by neutrons travelling at unaltered speed, their rarity among U_{238} isotopes meant that the target was much harder to locate. Conversely, the more plentiful U_{238} isotopes were far easier to locate with external neutrons, but the speed of some neutrons had to be artificially slowed down, or moderated, in order to prevent a neutron overload and a fizzle instead of fission.

This told physicists (and eventually atomic weapon makers) that they must either devise an industrial process to separate the two uranium isotopes and then distil the U_{235} into concentrations which allowed a viable critical mass, or instead find a means to artificially slow down neutrons and convert the U_{238} into much more potent plutonium.

Both routes to the atomic bomb presented unprecedented technical, industrial, and financial obstacles. No one knew if either highly enriched U_{235} or plutonium could be condensed and weaponized. To find out both options had to be tried, at enormous effort and cost.

In the spring of 1940, with Hitler now on the verge of capturing Paris and Nazi espionage agents scouring Europe for atomic ingredients, an embattled Winston Churchill was alerted and Britain soon convened a meeting of top scientists and military planners to thwart those efforts and build an atomic bomb first.

That would lead Britain, the U.S. and Canada to marshal forces for the famous Manhattan Project, eventually embed Ottawa in a web of international espionage, and give our nation the means to become an unwitting, then willing accomplice in atomic proliferation.

---

[19] This 1941 discovery is credited to American physicist Glenn Seaborg, who initially kept the first microgram sample of plutonium in his laboratory desk

On the eve of World War Two, no single country was capable of assembling the technical talent, materials, and industrial capacity to fashion a fission bomb. If national leaders and generals had gleaned any impression at all from the published reports in science journals, it was that atomic bombs might decide the outcome of the *next* major war.

But key physicists pressed on. Impelled by both intellectual thirst and the looming spectre of Nazi military might threatening Europe, Italy's brilliant Enrico Fermi emulated Einstein by emigrating to the U.S., several leading German physicists fled to Scandinavia, Niels Bohr found haven in England after a harrowing escape by plane,[20] and a small French team associated with Frederic Joliot-Curie prepared their own escape.

Earlier, the Paris experiments of Joliot-Curie, Lew Kowarski, Frances Perrin, Hans van Halban, and Bertrand Goldschmidt had confirmed that an exceedingly rare isotope of hydrogen had the unique ability to moderate the velocity of neutrons so that U_{238} could be converted into what proved to be plutonium. Code-named "polymer", it was formally known as deuterium, or heavy water.

These combined materials, the Paris group proved, could be used to produce 3.5 neutrons for every one aimed at the U_{238}. Harnessing this surplus would underpin one of two theoretical paths to a fission bomb, and the French team undoubtedly led all physicists in this critical sphere. Moreover, they had obtained access to the world's only source of heavy water, which was produced in small quantities at a hydro plant in remote Norway.

Events moved swiftly as Nazi Germany invaded Norway in early 1940, and advance troops moved to secure the heavy-water plant which supplied the German industrial chemical giant I.G. Farben. Weeks before, French interests acting for Kowarski had managed to smuggle out 26 cannisters. Later, with Churchill's help, Norwegian resistance fighters bombed the plant, and then sunk a barge containing barrels of heavy water heading for Berlin.[21]

---

[20] Bohr was strapped into the bomb-bay of a Mosquito warplane painted black on October 7, 1943 and barely survived the clandestine flight to Scotland.

[21] Because the French smuggled out the heavy water, British commando's sabotaged the production plant, and resistance fighters sunk the barge headed for Berlin, Nazi Germany lost any opportunity to produce plutonium. An inability to crack the secret of U235 enrichment effectively ended Hitler's attempt to acquire atomic bombs.

After the 185 kilograms reached Kowarski in Paris, he and Halban smuggled the heavy-water cannisters onto a British coal ship waiting in Bordeaux called the *Broompark*, then embarked on a clandestine exodus to England. Their hydrogen-rich cargo was first stashed in a prison, then with the Windsor Castle librarian.

When the French scientists joined their British colleagues at Cambridge, they comprised the leading atomic brain trust in the world. They also possessed the sole inventory of precious heavy water, and thus the best prospective path to producing plutonium. (Meanwhile, British efforts to distil U_{235} isotopes had barely crawled ahead due to daunting technical, financial and power supply hurdles, and competition for scarce war effort materials).

By comparison, despite brilliant individual talents, atomic research in Nazi Germany, the U.S. and especially Russia lagged months or years behind. And every country, including Britain, still lacked access to the most crucial component of all: secure access to large tonnages of uranium ore from which to glean either U_{235} or Pu_{239}.[22]

Nevertheless, the Cambridge team expanded in size, technical range, and influence. Promising physicists, chemists, engineers and graduate students were conscripted from British universities, industries and elite émigré ranks. Experiments accelerated, and expanded in scope, even as nightly Luftwaffe bombings of English cities intensified. Finally, as Paris fell to German forces, Prime Minister Winston Churchill authorized his high-level commission to secretly assess the research, and whether an atomic bomb could be built in time to be used as a military weapon against Hitler. The answer, delivered in July, 1941,[23] was contradictory.

The physicists predicted that a bomb with 5 kilograms of enriched U_{235} could equal the explosive force of several thousand tons of TNT - making that by far the most powerful weapon in history.[24] A plutonium bomb of comparable destruction was also possible. But military advisors countered that neither could be built without first importing hundreds of tonnes of uranium, and that such an effort might impair other wartime research and resources.

---

[22] The Germans seized a mine in Czechoslovakia which produced some uranium as a by-product, but it was never converted for production.
[23] The MAUD report.
[24] "Bomb Scare"; Cirincione; pg 2

Churchill had earlier rebuffed American requests for collaboration, but now concluded that if Britain could not build atomic bombs alone, the Anglo-Allies must. He personally implored President Roosevelt to join the clandestine effort, and add Canada as a source of uranium ore and temporary sanctuary for a transplanted British/French atomic team. Its explicit mission was to build a heavy-water reactor to produce bomb-grade plutonium.

To seal the deal, the eminent Cambridge scientist John Cockcroft was dispatched to personally brief sceptical American physicists and military advisors on the British atomic research. After a few uncertain and at times fractious months of negotiations, the secret plan was approved at the highest levels in London, Washington, and Ottawa.

What became the Manhattan Project had itself achieved critical mass.

By late 1942 members of the elite British/French atomic team in England were secretly shipbound for a vacant medical wing at the University of Montreal. It would become their secret research lab. The only drums of 99.5 per cent pure deuterium (heavy water) in existence arrived there later after a military bomber flight across the Atlantic.

Meanwhile, the leading American atomic team, based in Chicago, had just achieved a sustained nuclear chain reaction under the leadership of Enrico Fermi.[25] This breakthrough effectively erased the research lead of the Cambridge group, quickly shifting the Manhattan Project focus to U.S.-based U_{235} enrichment production in Tennessee, and to actual bomb design at Los Alamos in New Mexico.

Almost immediately, political frictions, personal rivalries, and paranoia threatened the Allied effort. American general-engineer Leslie Groves quickly dominated the Manhattan Project because only the U.S. had the money ($24 billion in current dollars) and industrial muscle to build the immense, costly plants needed. One Tennessee enrichment complex at Oak

---

[25] The world's first sustained chain reaction occurred December 2, 1942

Ridge covered 60,000 acres, and consumed as much power as the city of Cleveland.[26]

Inside both America and Canada, Groves controlled the budget, and all the Manhattan Project work plans, plant approvals, security clearances, scientific appointments, sub-contractors and information flows. His mission was a simple calculus: "If there are to be atomic weapons in the world, then we must have the best, the biggest, and the most."[27]

His command was implacable, bracingly candid, and routinely ruthless. This produced sparks from Fermi's group in Chicago (whom he alternately admired and derided as child-savants), and later at Los Alamos where J. Robert Oppenheimer led the bomb design teams.

Increasingly, it became clear to the British, French and Canadians that what Groves prized most was Canadian uranium ore deliveries from an orphaned mine in the forbidding Arctic tundra near Great Bear Lake, and the precious heavy water.[28] These were critical to pursing both the enriched U_{235} and plutonium routes to atomic fission.

Worse, Groves left little doubt that the Montreal team was slated to play only a supporting research role from a remote outpost. Experimental results began flowing south only. Security clearances were restricted, and sometimes revoked, especially for the non-British émigré's and those Groves suspected of socialist sympathies.

Manhattan Project memoirs and once classified memos confirm that Groves and his military attaché's planned from the outset to maintain a tight monopoly on key atomic secrets. This applied to Britain, France and Canada, but above all Nazi Germany, Japan and Communist Russia. To achieve this, he set up anti-espionage networks which included Montreal, authorized surveillance on even leading U.S. figures like Oppenheimer and

---

[26] The gaseous diffusion complex, which used miles of piping and centrifuges to separate U_{235} from U_{238}. It produced the enriched uranium used in the Hiroshima bomb.

[27] "Our Army of the Future", January, 1946

[28] When the Montreal group rebuffed Grove demands for the Norwegian heavy water, he ordered new supplies be made in Trail, British Columbia.

Fermi, and intercepted mail between British physicists based in Los Alamos and Washington.[29]

Groves harboured a particularly deep distrust of the French team in Montreal, despite their leading expertise in neutron marksmanship (known as 'capture rates'), and their daring effort to smuggle 185 kilograms of heavy water from Europe before it was seized by Nazis.

The trouble was that Hans van Halban, Frances Perrin, and Bertrand Goldschmidt were protégé's of the renowned scientist Frederic Joliot-Curie, who was an avowed communist. Groves dreaded the prospect of them relaying atomic secrets on to Joliot-Curie in Paris, who might in turn relay them on to Moscow.

In fact, they did have close personal ties with Joliot-Curie, but their deeper allegiance was to France. After the war, they convened in Paris and led the scientific effort to build atomic bombs. Replicating their specialized research in Canada, they created plutonium from a heavy water reactor originally designed in war-time Montreal. It was used in France's first atomic blast in 1960.[30]

Later, the French-Jewish chemist Goldschmidt, who first devised the technique for extracting plutonium from highly radioactive reactor wastes, would pass on these atomic secrets to Israel via a young intelligence officer named Shimon Peres. By 1968, Israel had constructed a clandestine heavy-water reactor to produce plutonium for its initial weapons stock.[31]

But in early 1943, the Montreal team protested their humiliating treatment by General Groves through diplomatic channels in Ottawa, Washington and eventually London. Then, with a rebellion pending, and the British-Canadian atomic effort starved of money and materials by Groves, Churchill himself insisted on a personal summit with Roosevelt and Canadian Prime Minister Mackenzie King to sort out the highly sensitive impasse.

After their meeting in Quebec City in August, 1943, the waters stayed relatively smooth. The secret settlement gave the U.S. prime responsibility

---

[29] Groves intercepted and read mail between physicist Rudolf Peirels in Los Alamos and James Chadwick, head of the British atomic delegation in Washington.
[30] This is documented in following chapters.
[31] "The Samson Option"; Seymour Hersh

for building the mammoth, expensive industrial plants needed to enrich U_{235}, build graphite-plutonium reactors,[32] and design and build the actual bombs. The Montreal mission was to produce plutonium from a prototype heavy-water moderated reactor, while Canada mined, refined and sent south the crucial uranium Groves required.

This placated Ottawa and most of the British and French scientists in Montreal, and chastened General Groves slightly. But it left Churchill privately furious, and embittered his relations with Roosevelt. He understood instantly that this garnered the U.S. the sole ability to make the initial bombs, and the infrastructure to sustain a post-war atomic *arsenal.*

As a global geo-political force, Churchill's beloved British Empire had just been eclipsed.

When the British/French team arrived in Montreal, they were welcomed by George C. Laurence, a Cambridge-trained Canadian physicist attached to the federal National Research Council. A specialist in radiation effects, Laurence had conducted his own intricate experiments with neutrons and uranium, and since 1940 had received detailed briefings on atomic research from leading U.S. and British scientists.

Though highly capable as a scientist and talent recruiter, Laurence was modest enough to recognize that many of the émigré scientists were already far ahead of his speculative research - particularly the French sub-unit headed by Hans van Halban. Using the precious heavy water smuggled from France, Halban and Kowarski had proved in Cambridge that it slowed or moderated neutrons and vastly increased the direct hits on U_{238} isotopes. That in turn produced fissile plutonium.

The military implications were clear. Ten kilograms of plutonium had the critical mass density to explode as a bomb, compared to 20 kilograms of U_{235}. Equally important, the plutonium path to the bomb eliminated the costly, technically daunting need to build mammoth industrial plants to enrich or distil rare U_{235} isotopes from plentiful U_{238} isotopes. Natural uranium would work perfectly.

---

[32] Using graphite as a neutron moderator, these reactors were constructed in Hanford in Washington state. They produced the plutonium used in the Nagasaki bomb.

But the plutonium route posed its own obstacles. A reactor capable of containing a sustained chain reaction would be required, as well as heavy-water distillation technology (modelled on the sabotaged Norwegian plant), and a special lab to chemically extract plutonium from intensely radioactive reactor wastes. Halban, Perrin and Goldschmidt had already delved deeply into these topics, and were primed to accelerate their plutonium-oriented research. Halban was chosen to head the scientific effort at the Montreal lab, while Laurence served as overall project director.

This did not sit well with General Groves, or some of the British team members in Montreal. The Manhattan Project director was convinced the French scientists were security risks, that U_{235} enrichment was the best route to a fission bomb, and that a graphite-moderated reactor might sooner produce plutonium than a heavy-water reactor.

Still, hedging his bets, Groves reluctantly approved the Halban work on condition all Canadian research results be copied to him for possible use in the U.S. He also formally insisted that the U.S. had absolute priority on all war-time uranium, heavy water, and graphite supplies coming from Canada. Soon after, citing security needs, exchanges and visits between the Montreal and U.S. scientists came to a virtual standstill.

These edicts caused intense resentment in Montreal, and left little doubt they were being pushed to the margins of the Manhattan Project. To make matters worse, Halban proved to be a bright mind but dismal leader. Arrogance and chaos marked his short tenure, and won little loyalty among the 300-member team - half of whom were Canadians.[33]

The tension reached a peak in late 1944. Halban made a surprise visit to newly liberated Paris to visit his communist mentor, Joliot-Curie. Ostensibly, it was to discuss commercial atomic patents Halban claimed to have negotiated with the British industrial firm ICI while he was at Cambridge.

But Groves was convinced the erratic Austrian was divulging atomic secrets, and that Halban's patent claims could confer commercial post-war atomic benefits to Britain's ICI (which was then partially funding the Montreal team) at the expense of an American competitor, du Pont, which Groves had already conscripted for similar work.

---

[33] "Early Decisions in the Development of the CANDU Program"; J. Lorne Gray; Atomic Energy of Canada

The visit to France enraged Groves, and doomed Halban's tenure as scientific leader in Montreal. He was forbidden to leave North America until the war ended, and du Pont replaced ICI as corporate contractor for the heavy-water research. Morale sank among all the scientists, and many began angling for transfers back to Cambridge, to the elite atomic team at Los Alamos, or to other pressing war-time scientific projects.

Despite the upheavals and loss of key talent like the Czech physicist George Plazcek to Los Alamos, the Montreal lab continued experiments on the heavy water/plutonium path to fission bombs.

The prescient and popular Lew Kowarski arrived from Cambridge to bolster the research of Halban, Perrin and Goldschmidt. Kowarski would soon take the lead in designing Canada's first reactor, a heavy-water plutonium producer called the NRX. Arriving from Chicago was Enrico Fermi's favoured protégé, Bruno Pontecorvo.[34] They were assisted by a growing corps of Canadians and promising émigré researchers. Among these was the British physicist Alan Nunn May, who was readily given access to the most secret research and fissile materials.

Pontecorvo was intimately involved in the war-time Montreal experiments which used heavy water to predict, then perfect, the efficiency with which neutrons converted U_{238} into Pu_{239}.[35] He was cleared to move between Manhattan Project sites, and carry confidential documents. He also arranged a brief 1944 trip to the remote Port Radium uranium mine in Canada's arctic, accompanied by Alan Nunn May, where he mapped out uranium ore bodies with a radiation detector he had invented.

Later, Pontecorvo would be part of the Kowarski team designing and building the NRX heavy-water reactor at Chalk River, Ontario. His key role from 1944-49 was to test neutron production and 'capture rates' as the shape of the lattice-reactor core was being designed and tested. Together with the plutonium extraction process developed by Bertrand Goldschmidt, the $4 million NRX would produce 17 kilograms of plutonium by the mid-

---

[34] Pontecorvo had won high honours as a student, and served the Fermi group in Italy with distinction on early key experiments with uranium. After Mussolini enacted anti-Jewish laws in Italy, he fled to the U.S. and re-joined Fermi in Chicago. Brilliant, genial and flamboyant, his nickname was "Cucciolo" - or 'puppy'.
[35] This occurs through a decay series involving uranium 239 and neptunium 239.

1950's [36] - proportionally more per tonne of uranium fuel than the first graphite-moderated reactors built by the U.S. military.

His work (and Goldschmidt's) was passed on to U.K. colleagues at Harwell, and earned him an important job offer there. However, he elected to remain in Chalk River until the NRX was operating. In his off-hours, he honed his tennis game to the point where he won a local singles title. In 1949, after more pioneering experiments in cosmic ray, neutrino and meson physics at Chalk River, the engaging, much admired Pontecorvo returned to post-war England, using his Canadian experience to obtain a top-security scientific posting at the Harwell atomic research complex. His research included intensified work on the design of a heavy-water reactor there. Better performance meant more plutonium.

In the late summer of 1950 he left for his native Italy for a family camping vacation, then disappeared. British security services tracked the family movements from Rome to Sweden, then Helsinki, then Moscow.[37]

According to a KGB agent memoir, Pontecorvo had been supplying atomic secrets to the Soviets since 1943, first from inside the Fermi group in Chicago, then from Montreal and Chalk River, then from Harwell. He was, by any account, a prize espionage catch. Until his death in 1993, his work in non-military theoretical physics, particularly neutrino's, continued to astound the world. That won Portecorvo an enduring place in the pantheon of modern physicists.

Nevertheless, his war-time secrets very likely helped Stalin's bomb team extract plutonium from heavy-water reactors based on those conceived in Canada. His uranium prospecting technology may also have helped Russia locate uranium ore bodies when an acute shortage crippled its efforts to build an arsenal with both atomic and hydrogen bombs. This may be why he was awarded the Stalin Prize in 1953.

Pontecorvo's defection was barely reported in Canada, and quickly erased from most public accounts of our early atomic research. Yet it was glaring proof that our first nominally peaceful Chalk River reactor (the NRX, which was later scaled up as the CANDU) was essentially an atomic bomb-factory design worthy of duplication by Josef Stalin.

---

[36] "Canada's Early Nuclear Policy"; Brian Buckley, pg 9
[37] "The Atom Bomb Spies"; H. Montgomery Hyde; 2003 historical research paper on Pontecorvo by Simone Turchetti

And by General Groves. Bending to diplomatic pressures, in April, 1944 he reluctantly approved building the prototype NRX heavy-water, natural uranium reactor in Canada. One condition was that the plutonium would be exclusively sold to the U.S., and thus offset the construction capital cost.

As an added *quid pro quo*, Hans van Halban was relegated to specialized physics work and Britain's legendary John Cockcroft was placed in direct charge of the Montreal contingent. Later, he would return to England to direct atomic research at Harwell, and personally enlist Bruno Pontecorvo and weapons physicist Klaus Fuchs to join his team there. Cockcroft would soon acutely regret approving their security clearances.

Groves was convinced the proposed NRX reactor could not be built in time to supply plutonium for a war-time weapon. He was right. But when the Chalk River plant soon after proved to be a prolific plutonium producer, the U.S. military purchased the entire Pu $_{239}$ output for its arsenal, and in the 1950's duplicate NRX heavy-water reactors (built by du Pont) were constructed in South Carolina to produce decades worth of weapons-grade plutonium.

The innate military advantage of the NRX reactor was obvious to Bruno Pontecorvo in 1944, and subsequently Laventrii Beria, the Russian dictator's brutal secret police chief. He also directed the global Soviet atomic espionage effort from his NKVD headquarters inside Moscow's infamous Lubianka prison. Later, Beria would personally direct Stalin's atomic bomb program.

Although Russia was then a member of the Allies, the Anglo-American leaders had all agreed that Moscow would be told nothing of their war-time atomic effort. Yet Beria knew of the Manhattan Project from the outset, and his agents relentlessly probed the Cambridge, Chicago, Oak Ridge and Los Alamos projects for leaks and weak links. Beria also placed secret agents in Ottawa and Montreal, who doubled as embassy attaché's, business agents or academics.[38]

Despite its explicit war-time mission, Ottawa officialdom apparently assumed the Montreal atomic research posed no security risks, and that Russia had proved itself a valiant, honourable ally. That illusion would be smashed exactly one month after the stunning atomic blast at Hiroshima.

---

[38] The extent of Beria's espionage network in Canada would soon be revealed by defector Igor Gouzenko, and a subsequent royal commission inquiry.

On the sunny morning of September 6, 1945, a barely coherent Russian cipher clerk named Igor Gouzenko suddenly appeared at the federal Justice building in Ottawa, seeking asylum. With him were his pregnant, tearful wife, and small son. When he insisted on seeing the Justice Minister himself, minor officials tried to shoo him away.

But gradually it was discerned that Gouzenko worked at the nearby Soviet embassy translating secret cables to and from intelligence headquarters in Moscow, and that he clutched documents in Russian script. They proved, he said, that Soviet espionage agents had burrowed deep into Canada's atomic research effort, and had spies planted in the cable-traffic de-coding rooms of our federal External Affairs headquarters, and the British High Commission in Ottawa.

That meant that many of the most sensitive war-time secrets shared between Ottawa, London and Washington were being routinely relayed to Moscow. Later, it would be confirmed that Stalin's NKVD and GRU operatives had not only obtained key atomic intelligence, but a small sample of coveted fissile material had already been hand-delivered to Beria personally in Moscow by a military attaché based in the Russian embassy in Ottawa.

Less than two hours after Prime Minister Mackenzie King was personally briefed about the Gouzenko charges by alarmed Justice and External Affairs senior deputies, his terse reply was relayed back to the officials left to deal with the Gouzenko's: "The prime minister has advised to get rid of these people at once."

That 'see-no-evil' response to troubling truths would soon bring on King's worst political nightmare, trigger the Cold War, and set the standard for Canada's nuclear proliferation policy for the next six decades.

ATOMIC ESPIONAGE

By the time the Canadian prime minister's message got back to the federal Justice building on Ottawa's Charlotte Street at mid-day, Gouzenko had disappeared.

Despite his increasing agitation, and warnings that he would be abducted by Soviet agents once they discovered him missing, Justice officials blithely advised him to go back to the Russian embassy. Gouzenko, accompanied by his frightened wife and bewildered child, protested that this would mean certain deportation, or death. Suicide, he said, would be better.

Unmoved, the Justice officials told Gouzenko the Minister would not see him. The terrified trio then left, and soon after Russian embassy agents were pounding on Gouzenko's apartment door. He escaped down the back stairs, and a neighbour alerted city police. That night, four more Russians returned and were caught ransacking the apartment, but were not charged after showing embassy credentials and claiming diplomatic immunity.

Meanwhile, King's priority was still to not offend the Russians - at virtually any cost. After his senior External Affairs advisor pointedly warned King that not granting immediate asylum might mean being a party to Gouzenko's suicide or murder, the prime minister replied that was not his concern.

"On no account take any initiative…My own feeling is that the individual has incurred the displeasure of the (Russian) Embassy, and is really seeking to shield himself. I do not believe his story about their avowed treachery."

This chilling verdict was given before any Justice or External Affairs officials examined or translated the cipher clerk's documents. Later that day, King would chat amiably with the Russian ambassador at a tea party.

But the midnight break-in at Gouzenko's apartment on September 6, 1945 changed his fate. While he was under protective police guard that night, Canada's most famous espionage figure, William "Intrepid" Stephenson, was alerted to the dramatic case. He was then chief of British overseas intelligence, but happened to be in Ottawa. Gouzenko was placed in RCMP care, and eventually given permanent asylum.

Within only days, while the Russian embassy demanded Gouzenko's return for "high crimes" and copies of the secret cables back to Moscow were translated, the first of the era's infamous atom bomb spies was identified. It was British scientist Alan Nunn May, code-named 'Alek', who had been transferred to Canada in 1943 from the Cambridge atomic research group.

The news stunned his Montreal lab director, John Cockcroft, who conceded to Ottawa's elite intelligence figures and King's senior staff that Nunn May knew most of the sensitive atomic secrets in both Canada and the U.S.

Studying the de-coded Russian cables, he told Stephenson that Nunn May was a top-flight physicist who "knew practically all about the current state of nuclear weapons research (and) had complete knowledge of the design of the Canadian heavy-water (reactor)...He knew the methods for separating plutonium and U_{235} and he could probably give the relative role of U_{235} and Pu_{239} in U.S. bombs."[39]

Cockcroft visibly blanched while reading translations of the Russian cables captured by Gouzenko, and Stephenson understood instantly the military meaning of the reference to heavy water. As a trusted war-time intelligence advisor to Churchill, he had suggested a commando bombing of the I.G. Farben plant in remote Norway, and arranged the 1943 airplane escape of Danish atomic physicist Niels Bohr to Scotland so he would not be captured by Nazis.

Both agreed heavy water was the route to plutonium - and the Russian's now knew it. The meeting took place in Ottawa at 2 a.m., days after the Gouzenko defection. Sworn to secrecy, Cockcroft returned to Montreal the next morning with instructions to steer Nunn May away from fissile materials and sensitive research without raising his suspicions.

Now all eyes turned to Stephenson. Was an immediate arrest wise due to the risk Nunn May could be tipped off by the NKVD about the Gouzenko defection and flee to Russia? Or should he be put under surveillance in order to expose a wider Russian espionage web?

At the time, Nunn May was then working in the Montreal lab on advanced atomic research, and scheduled to spend two weeks in Chalk River before returning to London for a university teaching post.

---

[39] Quote from "Intrepid's Last Case"; John Stevenson, page 86. The meeting was similarly described in "The Atom Bomb Spies", pages 23,24

"Intrepid" decisively argued for delaying his arrest. The Gouzenko documents showed that the Russian embassy in Ottawa alone controlled some two dozen operatives, and that hundreds of sensitive documents were being transmitted back to Moscow each week. They included details about atomic research, classified military specifications, and even copies of diplomatic cables between Washington, Ottawa and London.

This told him that America and England faced the same threat, and that Beria's espionage network might soon put Russia on atomic bomb parity with the U.S.

"Intrepid's" view held sway. Washington was alerted to the Gouzenko defection and the Nunn May case through the Canadian ambassador there, Lester Pearson. Stephenson also personally alerted FBI director Herbert Hoover,[40] General Groves, and his senior contacts in British Intelligence. Agreement was unanimous: Nunn May should be left to expose others, and all the Anglo intelligence agencies would be given access to the Gouzenko documents, and Gouzenko himself.

By marshalling forces this way, Stephenson became the lynchpin in future Allied anti-espionage efforts against the Russians, and the means to "stiffen the backbone" of a Canadian Prime Minister he scorned as a dithering,[41] dotty old *naïf* fond of talking to his deceased mother at night and consulting his dog for political advice.

When it was explained to King that arresting Nunn May immediately would inevitably single out Canada as a haven for atom spies, and preclude him garnering future credit for using daring patience to expose a wider Soviet espionage web, the pliable prime minister saw the light.

King would later write in his diary, "It can honestly be said that few more courageous acts have ever been performed (than) my own in the Russian intrigues against the Christian world."[42] Still later, when Moscow press and radio reports authorized by Stalin condemned King for granting Gouzenko asylum, he lamented: "The dispatches from Russia make clear that my name is now anathema throughout the whole Russian empire."

---

[40] Hoover wrote his top aides in mid-October, 1945 that following leads from the Gouzenko case was now the top FBI priority. "How the Cold War Began"; Amy Knight; pg 6

[41] King was once described as a statesman who did "nothing by halves-- which might be done by quarters."

[42] Mackenzie King diary, Feb 17, 1946

42

Torn between saving Christianity and befriending the Russian tyrant, King typically tried to choose both in the coming months.

As more Gouzenko documents were translated, the emerging details proved devastating. They confirmed that Nunn May knew of the secret Los Alamos bomb test in July, 1945, the components of the Hiroshima bomb, and that he had personally delivered fissile materials from the Montreal lab to Beria's Ottawa courier which then went to Moscow. The dates, names, and atomic materials were chillingly precise, and prompted immediate return cables from Moscow requesting more "technical processes, drawings, calculations."

This left no doubt that Stalin was accelerating his undeclared atomic weapons program, and that there were astute scientists in Russia compiling the espionage agent shopping lists.

When the new Nunn May revelations were relayed by encoded cable to U.S. President Harry Truman and new British Prime Minister Clement Atlee, their intelligence agencies intensified security investigations of their own atomic bomb personnel.

The Cold War had begun. By the end of September, 1945, prime minister King had given a personal Oval Office briefing on the Gouzenko documents to Truman, then sailed to England to do the same with Atlee. While in London - to the horror of those informed - King also sought spiritual guidance for his statesmanship during several séances. Then he made a surprise visit to the Russian embassy there to propose a personal meeting with Stalin to quietly settle the mutually embarrassing Gouzenko matter.

At the same time, the Russian embassy in Ottawa gave up trying to browbeat King's government into returning Gouzenko, and ceased attempted contacts with figures like Nunn May. In early December, 1945, a brigade of senior attaché's from the Russian embassy in Ottawa departed New York on the Russian steamer *Alexandrov* for an eventual rendezvous at Beria's intelligence headquarters in Moscow. The next stop for the leader of the disgraced group was a gulag in Siberia. [43]

---

[43] Knight; pg 100

43

While the Alan Nunn May fuse had been lit in early September, 1945, following the Gouzenko defection in Ottawa, Truman, Atlee and King were determined to delay the inevitable political detonation as long as possible.

Months passed as Nunn May returned to England without any signs of further espionage, and that gave King's government time to appoint a secret judicial panel, convened under the Official Secrets Act,[44] to marshal evidence for a pending royal commission and the expected resulting treason trials.

Gouzenko's documents, and the extensive testimony he was preparing in a carefully guarded hideout far from Ottawa, would form the body of evidence. Nunn May, now under constant surveillance in London, would be the prime prosecution target.

The delay also allowed U.S. intelligence figures like General Groves and FBI chief Herbert Hoover to scour domestic atomic operations for security leaks, and evidence of Russian espionage. The same applied in Britain. In both cases, using the Gouzenko documents and the NKVD links they contained, the atomic espionage trail led to famous results.

In America, this produced the Julius and Ethel Rosenberg convictions, then executions. There is now no doubt they sought and gave to Russian operatives information gleaned from the bomb project at Los Alamos. However, the crude diagrams and paltry technical detail failed to qualify as atomic secrets. In effect, their intent was treasonous, but what they delivered was militarily useless.

That was not the case with the U.K's notorious Klaus Fuchs. From 1941 to 1946, he routinely supplied Beria's agents in England and the U.S. with highly-sensitive atomic research involving uranium enrichment, plutonium production, final weapons designs, and even the ingredients needed for what became the hydrogen bomb.

---

[44] Modelled on the archaic, repressive British Official Secrets Act, it allowed King to order the arrest, imprisonment and interrogation of 13 suspects in Ottawa's Rockcliffe prison without charge, legal counsel, or access to any visitors including family for months.

None of this came from Canada, since Fuchs had only briefly toured the Montreal lab at the end of the war prior to his appointment as the head of theoretical physics at Britain's new Harwell atomic research site (where Pontecorvo joined him in 1949). But Fuchs had betrayed his country and colleagues as early as 1941 at the Cambridge atomic lab, while helping design the U.S. uranium enrichment plant at Oak Ridge, and from Los Alamos where he worked daily on bomb design with figures like Oppenheimer and Edward Teller.

Fuchs' treachery would bring treacherous results. In keeping with the *modus operandi* of his police chief Beria, Josef Stalin authorized the secret detonation of his first atomic bomb in August, 1949. It was detected weeks later by American and British planes taking high-atmosphere radioactive cloud samples, which were then drifting over Europe and the high arctic. At the same time, their intelligence agencies finally closed in on Fuchs by intercepting Russian diplomatic cables.

Confronted at his Harwell atomic research lab, Fuchs quietly submitted to extensive interrogation, readily confessed his treason in detail, pled guilty, and accepted the maximum sentence of 14 years imprisonment for violations of Britain's Official Secrets Act. On his release, he was deported to communist East Germany, where he was quickly awarded citizenship and a prized post at an atomic research centre.

Of all the nuclear spies, Fuchs himself later confessed that he abetted most Josef Stalin's drive to build his own atomic bomb, and likely Russia's first H-bomb. In his detailed confession, Fuchs identified the key role heavy-water (deuterium) and another variant called tritium would play in achieving thermonuclear explosions one thousand more times powerful than the bombs which had destroyed Hiroshima and Nagasaki.

From his Los Alamos work with Oppenheimer and Teller, Fuchs well understood that the secret to the H-bomb involved a carefully designed package of plutonium, enriched U_{235}, tritium-deuterium, and a key triggering device not used in A-bombs called lithium. In essence, the H-bomb would be a contained fission-fusion-fission reaction which took place in millionths of a second.

The technical details of the Fuchs confession were not released at his trial, nor publicly for decades. But they were immediately passed on to select British, U.S. and Canadian intelligence figures. So each nation knew in 1950 that a weapon even more terrifying than the atomic bomb might soon be built, and its ingredients would be plutonium, uranium, tritium, deuterium, and lithium.

Soon all these would be exported from Canada to U.S. military sites as President Harry Truman raced to beat Josef Stalin to the H-bomb.

The autumn, 1945, delay in arresting Allan Nunn May allowed all three Allied governments to brace for an inevitable political and public uproar. It would be the first the world heard of atom bomb spies.

That came in mid-February, 1946, when thirteen people were arrested in Canada, and the King government announced Gouzenko's defection and its related espionage inquiry. This put Canada's capital in an uproar and drew intense press coverage from around the world. Not a little chagrin dampened the *Ottawa Journal* newsroom, where an editor had months earlier shown Gouzenko the door after concluding his defection was "no story".

Now under fire, King rose in Canada's Parliament to defend the arrests. With breath-taking bravado, he conferred credit on himself for smashing a perfidious Soviet spy ring - and then claimed Stalin was likely innocent in the affair.

"What I know or have learned of Mr. Stalin from those who have been closely associated with him in the war causes me to believe he would not countenance action of this kind on the part of officials of his country," he told the House of Commons. "I believe when these facts are known to him and others in positions of full authority, we shall find that a change will come that will make a vast difference indeed."

Behind the scenes, ever obsessed with deflecting damage, King waited on tenterhooks for news of Nunn May being captured in England, not Canada. He was finally arrested without incident, without exposing any Russian agents, in late February, 1946.

After first denying any espionage or contacts with Russians, Nunn May cracked when confronted with the evidence in the Ottawa-Moscow embassy cables Gouzenko had stolen. While refusing to disclose the names of his Russian contacts, he admitted supplying agents with fissile samples, and summary reports on atomic research from Montreal and Chicago until

46

August, 1945. After pleading guilty at a very brief trial, he was sentenced to 10 years in prison for dispensing atomic secrets.

While Mackenzie King garnered prestige and praise with the Nunn May 'atom spy' conviction in England, it became evident that the espionage charges back in Canada would soon reap political trouble. None involved atomic secrets. Some involved minor, pitiful figures. A half dozen men had passed on military specifications, of limited value, when Russia was an official ally. The one exception was the sensational conviction of a sitting Member of Parliament, the Montreal communist Fred Rose.

But many other charges proved wild and baseless, dozens of innocent lives were badly damaged, and violations of legal due process were rampant. In perhaps the most senseless case, the brilliant Canadian mathematician Israel Halperin was imprisoned without charge for months, despite a written plea for his release from former Princeton University colleagues - including Albert Einstein. He was charged but acquitted after it was proved he had rejected all Soviet entreaties to divulge secrets.

Stung by the mounting public outcry about these cases, King began crafting domestic and international atomic policies designed to distance Canada from the spectre of Hiroshima and cleanse the security stigma of atom bomb spies.
During the war, Ottawa had embraced joining the Manhattan Project, accepted U.S. payments for uranium, heavy-water and graphite exports, benefited from the infusion of talented transplanted scientists serving a military mission, and obtained important support from General Groves for the NRX reactor project. In the days following the Japan blasts, King had made sure Canada garnered credit for its contribution.

Now it wanted to be a boy scout. Canada's role in the Manhattan Project was adroitly eclipsed by a diplomatic declaration that it would not build nuclear weapons. And, despite the explicit military genesis of the Chalk River reactor, the King government was now careful to describe the NRX as a paragon of peaceful nuclear research. Later, the scaled-up CANDU would be pitched the same way.

But the NRX was, as planned, a prolific plutonium producer from the day it went critical. As the *quid pro quo* for financing its construction, virtually all that bomb-grade product was shipped to the U.S. military until copies of the NRX reactor were built in South Carolina by the du Pont Corporation. And Canada, through the federal crown corporation Eldorado Nuclear, continued to sell increasing amounts of uranium for use in the growing

American arsenal. (The first civilian atomic plant in the U.S. did not open until 1958).

These military exports increased even as Lester Pearson, now the newly-appointed Canadian minister of External Affairs, joined his American and British counterparts in drafting an international protocol for preventing atomic proliferation. The laudable idea was that nations would renounce the acquisition of atomic weapons, and agree to stockpile all fissile materials under the control of a U.N. entity. If future peaceful uses were found, they would be solely supplied by that agency.

The protocol, which took shape as the Acheson-Lillienthal proposal, had great merit. It was eventually supported by many countries and eminent scientists - including many who had been involved in the Manhattan Project. Canada became one of the first nations to endorse this protocol politically, by formally foreswearing the development of atomic weapons.

It was a fine diplomatic gesture, with a sound technical grounding.

In the days following the Japanese blasts, the Truman government had released an independent, expert report summarizing as precisely as possible (without breaching security) how the Manhattan Project had succeeded. Authored by Princeton professor Henry D. Smyth, it was intended to inform the President, his advisors, U.S. military leaders, Congress, diplomats, and other scientists about atomic bomb basics, and help meld effective future policies. From it emerged the Acheson-Lillienthal proposal.

Known as the Smyth Report, it meticulously examined the basic physics involved, the nature of fissile materials, and the important role of isotopes like heavy-water (deuterium). No one challenged Smyth's credibility, the Smyth Report science, nor his survey of what technology was involved in building nuclear bombs, and what scientific and physical resources nations would require to succeed.
But Smyth's conclusions were stark: nothing but *intent* separated military and peaceful atoms; and only a strictly enforced international quarantine on fissile materials could prevent proliferation to countless nations. This posed a very inconvenient truth, and a clear, uncompromising model for non-proliferation.

It was not welcomed in Washington, London, Moscow, and Ottawa. Despite some lofty diplomatic declarations about avoiding an atomic arms race, each nation privately pursued exactly the opposite. As fast as possible.

48

Between 1945 and 1949, the U.S. accelerated atomic bomb production, Britain secretly approved plans to create an arsenal of 200 weapons by 1952, Russia raced to build its first weapon by 1949, and Canada ramped up plans to export uranium, plutonium, and heavy-water for American and British arsenals.

Soon these military imperatives, and a nascent effort to cash in on future commercial sales of nuclear technology and fuels, would be cloaked in a public-friendly international initiative called "*Atoms for Peace*". This raised great hopes among many scientists, politicians, and the public. What better way to expiate the harrowing example of Hiroshima than by turning nuclear swords into ploughshares?

But the Smyth Report had lucidly warned that the spread of nominally peaceful atoms would inevitably foster military use - not stop it. This proved tragically accurate when governments and nuclear boosters began deliberately denying the true nature of atomic physics.

It was at that point that mistaken belief descended into duplicity, and countries like Canada became accomplices in the very proliferation they pledged to stop.

Building the first atomic bomb required four years of the most concerted scientific and industrial effort ever marshalled in human history, $2 billion, and the united political and military will of three Allied nations.

Josef Stalin detonated a pirated copy four years later. When U.S. President Harry Truman was told that airplanes had picked up radioactive proof in high-altitude clouds weeks after the August, 1949 blast, his first disbelieving question was: "Are you sure? Are you *sure?*"

Truman's gut reaction was gall. Many of his military and scientific advisors had assured him it would take Russia a decade or more to build a bomb. He was sure essential secrets had been stolen by Beria's espionage ring - in what amounted to the most brazen case of intellectual theft in human history.

And, perhaps worse, Stalin had feigned no interest in atomic weaponry when "a tremendously pepped up" Truman had hinted, during the July, 1945 Allied Powers summit in Potsdam, Germany, that America might soon use a new superweapon against Japan. There was a reason for Truman's ebullient mood. Eight days earlier, Oppenheimer's team had detonated the *Trinity* plutonium bomb at Alamagordo, New Mexico. The 'yield' had been equivalent to 20,000 tonnes of TNT.

So when Stalin's 1949 counter-punch came in the form of a knock-off plutonium bomb with *twice* the explosive yield, it hit home hard. It took Truman weeks to compose himself enough to acknowledge the news publicly.

Then it was the world's turn to be stunned. Russia had barely emerged from a war in which Hitler's armies had reached the outskirts of Moscow, and been repelled at an eventual cost of 20 million lives. It was still an essentially agrarian nation, crippled by debt, drought, famine and decrepit infrastructure. Russia's national treasury was depleted, and its survival was thought to rest on hard labour, not high science.

But suddenly and literally, in a flash of fissioned plutonium, it had acquired geo-political parity with America.

It would take decades for western intelligence sources to penetrate the Kremlin-sealed society, and piece together a precise picture of how Stalin had succeeded. Even U-2 spy planes and satellites could barely discern where and how Russia's growing nuclear arsenal was produced.

But a precise picture was not needed. A reading of the Smyth Report could identify the ingredients. Some would blame this publication for Stalin's perverse success. Yet it only summarized secrets which had already escaped, and predicted that any group of talented scientists and engineers could - sooner or later - coax them from the revealed laws of physics.

In Russia's case, the secrets treasonously stolen by Fuchs, or passed on by Nunn May and quite likely Pontecorvo, hastened the Soviet detonation by a few years at most. Once Hiroshima had proven it possible, it was inevitable that Russia's most talented scientists would deduce how.

But what made it happen so soon was Stalin's obsession to build an A-bomb at any cost. The decisive moment came with the dramatic atomic bombings of Japan, and the promotion of Laventrii Beria - two weeks later - from secret police chief to commander of Russia's bomb project.

The promotion was both cruelly ironic, and brilliant. Beria himself had decimated the ranks of top Russian physicists in earlier anti-intellectual purges ordered by Stalin. Many others had been sent to forced labour camps, stripped of research and teaching posts, or driven into exile.

Now Beria had to assemble those scientists who remained, and overcome formidable technical barriers. Russia then had no domestic uranium mines. The U_{235} enrichment puzzle had to be solved, then massive plants built. Only a handful of adequate labs existed. It had no means to produce the heavy water or pure graphite needed for a plutonium production reactor.

But it had a corps of immensely talented scientists who had kept apprised of western advances in physics until the war, and now knew an atomic bomb had exploded. Beria promised them that money, materials, engineering talent, labs, industrial infrastructure and mass labour on a Manhattan Project scale would be provided on demand. But he also made it plain that the penalty for failure would be death or deportation to Siberia.

One scientist who led Russia's atomic bomb effort was Iulii Khariton, who had earned his PhD at the Cambridge physics lab in England under the legendary mentors Rutherford and Chadwick. The other was Igor Kurchatov, director of Soviet atomic arsenal production from 1943 to 1960.

Both men had learned of the Meitner and Frisch chain reaction discovery weeks after it was published in early 1939. Only months later, Kharition authored a paper with a prescient conclusion: "It is necessary to use heavy hydrogen (deuterium) or, perhaps, heavy water or some other substance which will ensure a small enough capture cross-section [ie probability of capture] in order to slow down the neutrons…The other possibility consists in enriching uranium with the isotope $_{235}$."[45]

This makes it obvious that two years *before* the Manhattan Project was authorized, Russian scientists had already deduced the two routes to the bomb, and the essential materials required. By September, 1940, an expert team had been assembled to solve the physics puzzles, and Beria had operatives vainly searching for 2.5 tonnes of uranium metal and 15 tonnes of heavy water.

The scarcity of uranium and heavy water left the Russian physicists to conduct their experiments on a micro scale, and the problem worsened when Hitler's armies invaded Russia. Atomic research began faltering badly. Then the cunning Beria hit upon a way to eliminate much of that required research - by stealing it from the Allies.

Now declassified Russian documents show that as early as September, 1941, NKVD agents in England had obtained copies of the secret, technically explicit report Churchill received recommending an atomic bomb effort be approved. It confirmed there were two routes to the bomb: U$_{235}$ and plutonium. Soon after, Moscow began receiving atomic secrets from Klaus Fuchs in England, then from his posts in America after 1943.

Beria passed this intelligence on to his top scientists, and Stalin. From it, the Russian scientists gleaned crucial information, such as the critical mass required for a bomb, which saved months and possibly years of effort. In February,1943, Kurchatov met with Stalin's formidable Foreign Affairs minister, Molotov, at the Kremlin. After expressing doubts about whether a bomb could be made quickly, Molotov gave the scientist a compendium of espionage reports filed from agents in England.

Kurchatov was stunned. He spent days reading the detailed NKVD summaries, which he described as having "huge, inestimable significance for our state and science…It has made it possible to by-pass very labour-intensive phases of working out the problem." The most important secret,

---

[45] "Stalin and the Bomb"; David Holloway, pg 53

he concluded, was the outline of British research on fission related to *heavy water*. It was the surest, fastest way to a bomb.

But with only some two kilograms in all of Russia, he needed more heavy water and foreign experimental data. Kurchatov immediately asked Beria to somehow provide both. The NKVD soon discovered that the French heavy water experts - and the only known stock of actual heavy water - were now in Montreal.

This largely explains why Stalin had some twenty NKVD and GRU agents stationed at the Russian embassy in the otherwise sleepy capital of Ottawa from 1943-1945, probing for ways to penetrate the heavy water research related to the Chalk River reactor. They found their quarry in Nunn May and Pontecorvo. The urgency of this task is conveyed in a secret cable the director of military intelligence in Moscow sent Ottawa on August 22, 1945 - just prior to the Gouzenko defection:

"Take measures to organize acquisition of documentary materials on the atomic bomb! The technical process, drawings, calculations." [46]

But Beria's brazenness did not stop there. Once Russia became a war-time member of the Allies, it was routinely provided with American war materials under the Lend-Lease Agreement. In 1943, Russia asked for 420 kilograms of metallic uranium, which was delivered in two shipments approved by General Groves.[47] Russia was also allotted 1,100 grams of heavy water that November. Given his obsessions about atomic security, it seems incredible that the Manhattan Project commander would allow the export of such materials to any country, let alone Russia. There could be only one logical purpose for them. But apparently Groves believed that a refusal would telegraph America's own military interest in uranium and heavy-water, and thus incite Stalin.

Groves may have been too clever by half. By then, Fuchs was giving Russian agents technical reports on U_{235} separation technology at Oak Ridge, and would soon provide the most explicit details on plutonium bomb design and detonation techniques.

By late 1943, Kurchatov was confident enough to convene his own bomb design team, and Beria approved the construction of a remote Ural region atomic complex called Cheliabinsk-40. It eventually contained Russia's first

---

[46] Royal Commission Report (Gouzenko inquiry) 1946, page 452
[47] ibid, page 101

53

plutonium-production reactor, a plutonium separation plant, and a large heavy-water reactor used to sustain the future Soviet atomic and hydrogen bomb arsenal with plutonium. Building the complex required 70,000 prisoner-labourers, most of whom later disappeared into gulags so Stalin could preserve the 'hidden city' status of Cheliabinsk-40.

On Christmas night, 1946, the first sustained chain reaction took place there as Kurchatov declared: "Atomic power has now been subordinated to the will of Soviet man."

By June, 1949 there was enough plutonium[48] for a first atomic bomb. With Laventrii Beria watching, it was detonated on August 29, in the desolate steppes of Kazakhstan. It would be the first of more than 450 test blasts at the site. As a mushroom cloud formed overhead, Stalin's sinister lieutenant annointed Kurchatov and Khariton with a kiss on their foreheads.

It was a chilling scene - not least because despite his vital role in the bomb project, Khariton had been spied on by Beria informants due to his past ties to Cambridge scientists, and the fact that he was Jewish. His journalist father had previously disappeared after being arrested by Stalin's secret police.
Nevertheless, Khariton would later recall: "When we succeeded in solving this problem, we felt relief, even happiness - for in possessing such a weapon we had removed the possibility of its being used against the USSR with impunity."

Thus the defensive military calculus of mutually assured destruction was born. But it wrought just the opposite of national security.

When Russia's first bomb was tested, America held an apparently invincible lead in atomic arsenal development.

A year after the *Trinity* explosion in New Mexico, in July, 1946 it tested two bombs on the Bikini atoll in the Pacific as part of a plan to devise more

---

[48] This plutonium was derived from a small graphite moderated reactor. Russia's heavy water distillation plant and heavy water plutonium production reactor were not yet ready.

efficient weapons. By then, the U.S. arsenal had nine bombs. That rose to thirteen the next year, then 56 by 1948, then 200 by 1950.[49]

Monopolies are widely reviled except by those that have them, and in the year preceding Russia's first atomic blast U.S. President Truman saw little incentive to relinquish his. Earlier, in the weeks before Hiroshima, he had rejected appeals by some Manhattan Project scientists[50] to try a Pacific island test bomb blast before international witnesses to compel Japan's quick surrender, or at least use the weapons only on military targets.

Now, to avert a potential atomic arms race, a growing scientific and diplomatic chorus was pressing for the creation of an international body to quarantine and control all fissile materials. The inaugural session of the United Nations had earlier created a commission to accomplish this, and sought state-to-state implementation accords.

By 1948, negotiations had reached an apparent high-water mark. Many prominent scientists - including Einstein, Oppenheimer and Niels Bohr - publicly and privately appealed for the superpowers to accede. Their plea was doomed. By then, London, Moscow and Washington had, behind carefully crafted diplomatic camouflage, voted on their international proliferation policies with their domestic military budgets.

In February, 1946, the British had shocked their American and Canadian atomic partners by declaring that its Montreal contingent would be hauled home, and begin constructing a large-scale plutonium production reactor.[51] The obvious was left unsaid.

On January 8, 1947, British Prime Minister Clement Attlee and his inner cabinet secretly approved its own atomic bomb program, with a goal of several hundred weapons by 1957. Modelled on the Manhattan Project and spread over multiple sites, it was to produce an arsenal of both enriched U_{235} and plutonium bombs, and eventually H-bombs.

But there was no location on the British Isles suitable for a bomb test - so England looked to the colonies. The top scientist conscripted to conduct the tests initially selected seven sites in Canada, including Churchill,

---

[49] "Bomb Scare"; Cirincione; pg 21
[50] Led by Noble Laureate James Franck, who had worked with Enrico Fermi in Chicago.
[51] "Canada's Early Nuclear Policy", pg 61

Manitoba, to detonate Britain's first dozen atomic bombs. But offshore Australia proved more attractive.[52]

Despite the crippling post-war economic crisis in England, and its reliance on the U.S. government for loans and credits to stay solvent, the bomb program accelerated at great expense. The first plutonium was produced in early 1952. But there was not enough for Britain's October test blast on the Montebello Islands of Australia, so it formally asked Canada for 5 kilograms.

Canada agreed, but the U.S. - determined to thwart or delay Britain's entry into the nuclear club - insisted it had pre-contracted all the Chalk River plutonium for its own military use. Canada finessed the impasse by 'lending' the U.K a lesser amount.[53] It went into the first British atomic bomb, which was proudly approved by a re-elected Winston Churchill. The previous year, during a personal visit to Ottawa, he had advised Lester Pearson of the pending event.[54]

Meanwhile, as Stalin's foreign minister Molotov promoted non-proliferation protocols at the U.N., his secret police chief Beria was masterminding Russia's bomb effort. At a 'secret city' in the Ural region named after him, an entire weapons complex was built in just 18 months, from which Russian plutonium bombs were made for the next four decades. The complex included a heavy-water reactor similar to the Chalk River design, which began construction in 1948.

As early as 1946, Truman had concluded: "Unless Russia is faced with an iron fist and strong language another war is in the making. I'm tired of babying the Russians." His subsequent federal departmental spending (which had a multi-year lag effect) saw atomic warhead production increase exponentially, from 56 in 1948 to 298 in 1950 to 1,161 in 1953. During the same period, warhead capable long-range bomber numbers climbed from 30 to 1,000. [55]

Thus, in the decade since Christmas, 1938, when the theoretical physicist Lise Meitner had first intuited the neutron chain reaction, the physical fate of the atom had shifted from scientists to politicians and generals. As had the moral pivot-point.

---

[52] Gowing, Margaret; "Independence and Deterrence"; pgs 477-78
[53] "Canada's Early Nuclear Policy"; pg 95
[54] ibid, pg 107
[55] Bulletin of Atomic Scientists; March, 1993

Perhaps no single scene symbolized this more vividly than a post-war exchange between President Truman and Manhattan Project leader J. Robert Oppenheimer. It took place on the eve of the U.N.'s first conference on atomic disarmament.

Perhaps in partial atonement for his role in the Japanese bombings, and anxious to avert a pending arms race with Russia, Oppenheimer supported future U.N. control of fissile materials. Truman stubbornly opposed the idea, then took deep offense when an anguished Oppenheimer suddenly bared the moral issue by blurting out: "Mr. President - I have blood on my hands!"

Afterward, Truman told the senior aide who had arranged the meeting: "Don't you bring that fellow around again. After all, all he did was make the bomb. I'm the guy who fired it off."[56]

---

[56] "Oppenheimer: Father of the Bomb", Peter Goodchild, pg 172

MONOPOLIES AND MIXED MOTIVES

When World War Two ended, Canada was the dominant uranium producer in the western world, and virtually every ounce was sold under export contract to the U.S. military. The seller was Ottawa itself since, under the War Measures Act, it had summarily expropriated the single uranium mine and refining plant in Canada in early 1944.

Even so, the war-time shipments had amounted to less than 1,000 tonnes. That would prove to be a fraction of future demand for the U.S. and British atomic arsenals. Thus, Ottawa's position left it poised to reap rich future benefits for the federal treasury, while also buttressing an intended Allied monopoly on atomic arms production.

No one had anticipated this more acutely than Manhattan Project commander Leslie Groves. In early 1943, he had set up a secret Army operation, code-named *Murray Hill Area* [57], to scout out and buy every viable uranium deposit in the world. Neither the Canadians nor the British were told.

Groves had carte blanche from President Roosevelt to spend up to $60 million per month on Manhattan Project expenses,[58] which included $37 million deposited into his personal bank account [59]. He used this fund, in part, to covertly purchase uranium claims adjacent to Canada's high arctic mine, and contract for all of Eldorado's uranium production. He also had intelligence agents wire-tap its Port Hope refinery offices, and secretly surveilled company officials. Ottawa was not informed.[60]

At the same time, Groves imposed an undeclared embargo on uranium supplies requested by the Montreal atomic research team. Repeated pleas for even a few tonnes went unheeded. This dismayed the Canadians, but sent the British ballistic. Intent on securing its own monopoly on Canadian uranium, they suddenly gleaned (from their own intelligence sources) that their American ally was conniving to monopolize uranium not only for the bomb effort, but post-war use.

---

[57] Named after the New York City telephone exchange where Groves had his headquarters.
[58] "Oppenheimer: The Father of the Bomb", pg 55.
[59] "Atomic Audit"; Stephen I. Schwartz; page 40
[60] "Eldorado: Canada's National Uranium Company: Robert Bothwell; pgs 117-154

58

Assuming the Canadians had consented, Churchill thundered Ottawa was "selling the British Empire down the stream." He sent an emissary directly to Roosevelt to report the betrayal, who cheerfully replied that the misunderstanding would be rectified at the upcoming Allied summit in Quebec City.

In the interim, Groves placed a telephone call to Canada's federal minister of munitions, C.D. Howe, and suggested a secret briefing in Ottawa. The scene was set for a fiery showdown.

The bellicose Groves wielded total control over Manhattan Project expenditures and supplies, had just conducted a covert operation inside the borders of its ally, and now was refusing to sell Canadian uranium to the Montreal contingent of the Manhattan Project. Howe was a formidable, hard-nosed industrialist himself, and the pre-eminent cabinet minister who directed hundreds of domestic and British war plants in Canada. In both cases, their opinions often became the conclusions of the presidents and prime minister they served.

But the two titans took to each other instantly, and a two-hour meeting settled the impasse. Soon after, on national security grounds, Howe issued a federal statute declaring all uranium deposits in Canada would henceforth be owned by the federal government. Ottawa began buying up Eldorado shares, then nationalized its mine and refinery in 1944.

With Ottawa now holding a monopoly on all uranium production in Canada, Howe approved contracts sending all war-time shipments to America, except 100 tonnes for the Canadian-British work in Montreal. Problem solved - except for the pending conflict-of-interest which put Ottawa's prospective uranium export sales squarely at odds with post-Hiroshima atomic proliferation proposals to strictly limit them.

Soon a key individual would be caught squarely between these two opposing imperatives: future Noble laureate and Canadian prime minister Lester Pearson.

Although J. Robert Oppenheimer resigned from his Manhattan Project duties months after Hiroshima, General Groves did not. In August, 1945 he presided over a newly-minted, $2 billion industrial juggernaut that had its own formidable mass and velocity. It comprised some 30 plants in a dozen U.S. states, and employed 130,000.

Only one thing could bring it to a dead halt: no uranium. With negligible known deposits in the U.S., Groves looked north to Canada. It had the only operating mine and refinery in the western world.

Using continued support for the Chalk River NRX reactor as leverage, he demanded exclusive access to all Canadian uranium production. This would secure supplies - and neatly cut out the British, who reacted with predictable fury. The temporary truce attained by Churchill and Roosevelt vanished, and in part incited prime minister Attlee to secretly approve building a replica of the Manhattan Project complex in England.

Now Ottawa was caught between two imposing countries acting like anything but Allies. Nevertheless, its uranium assets proved to be a perfect - and highly profitable - example of the value of 'location, location, location'. The two rivals drove the price up.

For the newly nationalized Eldorado Nuclear, and thus Ottawa, initial post-war uranium sales to the U.S. proved highly profitable, and paid for the prospecting for new mines in northern Saskatchewan. Even though the price doubled from 1945 to 1950, every pound of uranium was pre-sold.

Although details of these U.S. contracts were kept secret, Mackenzie King's top external affairs official, Lester Pearson, knew them intimately. He had endorsed the state-to-state uranium supply agreements even while he was crafting Ottawa's diplomatic position on atomic arms control.

Only two months after Hiroshima, the Canadian director of the Montreal atomic team had lucidly warned Pearson and his staff that no future monopoly on uranium, plutonium production, or atom bomb design was possible. Only U.N. control of all fissile materials could avert an atomic arms race.

This echoed the science-based Smyth Report, and was reflected in a secret memo Pearson wrote for prime minister King on the eve of his White House meeting with Truman in November, 1945.

"Unless there is agreement between nations regarding atomic bomb there will be competition. Such competition would be the most bitter and disastrous armament race ever. Any constructive solution ...must be international - not national. There is, in fact, no national solution... With

60

the atomic bomb suspended over our heads, it would be madness not to attempt (this)."[61]

But King did not make this case to Truman, and so cemented the bi-polar disorder embedded in Canada's main atomic policies. One sought to accelerate uranium exports destined solely for bomb production, the other to confine all uranium production to a proposed U.N. agency for strictly peaceful uses. But there was then no market for fuelling civilian reactors - they did not exist.

Torn between profitable uranium exports to the U.S. (and soon the British military) and wanting a strong anti-proliferation presence at the U.N., Pearson spent most of 1948 assuring a compliant, undoubtedly confused Mackenzie King that both were possible.[62]

But when Russia overthrew democratic Czechoslovakia and imposed the East Berlin blockade, atomic arms control policies quickly lost diplomatic *gravitas* in Washington, London and Ottawa. When Stalin detonated Russia's first bomb in August, 1949, what little remained was vapourized.

If Pearson was personally conflicted by the glaring disconnect between Canadian military uranium sales and global atomic arms control, that would magnify with his election to public office. As a Mackenzie King Liberal, he won the northern Ontario riding of Algoma East in 1948, which included the industrial steel city of Sault. Ste. Marie.

Pearson was immediately appointed to the King cabinet as minister of External Affairs. Few could question his credentials. He had been Canadian ambassador to Washington during the war, provisional head of the nascent U.N., and deputy minister of External Affairs.[63] He knew his subject, and all the main diplomatic and intelligence figures in Ottawa, Washington, and London.

Pearson also knew the Gouzenko and uranium files in detail, and that both had left battle scars on King and C.D. Howe. Stalin's now exposed bomb program, and the sensational atom spy trials of Alan Nunn May and Klaus

---

[61] Ambassador Pearson's memo was dated November 8, 1945

[62] King was well past age 70, and his days as prime minister were numbered.

[63] The most senior civil service position.

Fuchs soon incited the U.S. and Britain to demand more and more uranium. The affable, ambitious new cabinet minister was happy to assist, even though Pearson knew the new U.S. orders would in part be destined for weapons far more terrifying than mere atomic ones.

The day after the January, 1950 confession of Soviet scientist-spy Klaus Fuchs in England, Oppenheimer and Los Alamos bomb designer Edward Teller personally advised their President that Fuchs knew every essential secret of the hydrogen bomb.[64] The next day, Truman authorized a crash program to build a thermonuclear weapon, and acquire all the related ingredients: uranium, plutonium, deuterium, tritium and a trigger component called lithium.

Soon all would be secretly supplied by Canada.

The Truman H-bomb directive saw funding for the U.S. Atomic Energy Commission (USAEC) rise from $260 million in 1950 to $1 billion the following year, to $5 billion in 1952. As a result, nuclear warhead totals climbed from 1,000 in 1953 to 18,000 by 1960.[65] The military demand for uranium also drove up prices, prospecting for uranium deposits surged, and new, richer deposits were discovered in Canada and western U.S. states.

In November, 1952, the U.S. detonated its first hydrogen bomb in the south Pacific. Contained inside a 65-ton, refrigerated metal structure, its explosive force was 500 times that of the Hiroshima bomb. The island it was built on vapourized, and the blast jigged seismographic meters in San Francisco. Some witnesses feared that the fireball might ignite hydrogen in the atmosphere.

The U.S. lead in the thermonuclear race lasted mere months. In August, 1953, the Russians detonated a smaller, but more efficient device code-named Joe One in honour of the recently deceased dictator, Stalin. It had a second chilling refinement: unlike the first U.S. fusion bomb, it was compact enough to be delivered by a long-range bomber. More powerful H-bomb tests soon followed.

That incited Truman to accelerate the pace of building the U.S. atomic and hydrogen bomb arsenal, and acquire even more uranium. For the first time, private companies were encouraged to finance and build uranium mines,

---

[64] "Oppenheimer", pages 195, 196
[65] "Eldorado"; Bothwell; pg 237

62

but with the strict proviso that the only purchasers would be either the U.S. military, or Canada's crown company, Eldorado.

Eldorado's strategic status also allowed Ottawa to supply Britain where - despite strong objections from Washington - its own atomic bomb complex had been completed. Using uranium obtained via Belgium and plutonium from Chalk River, it detonated its first A-bomb in Australia in 1952. Its first H-bomb was tested in May, 1957.

That flattened American resistance, and Canada (via Eldorado) soon negotiated major uranium supply contracts with Britain which eventually totalled 10,500 tons. At the time the U.K. had no civilian reactors, and no proliferation safeguards were written into the contracts. External Affairs minister Lester Pearson sat on the federal cabinet uranium sub-committee which approved these exports.

Flush with cash, the federally-owned Eldorado found and developed a major deposit at Beaverlodge in far northern Saskatchewan. That soon produced several lucrative satellite mines and a remote boom town called Uranium City. A similar rush to riches occurred in Colorado. Virtually all the uranium ended up in U.S. bomb production plants. Yet demand for uranium was still not slaked.

Despite this, in April, 1954, then External Affairs minister Lester Pearson assured the House of Commons: "Although Canada was a partner in the war-time project to develop atomic weapons, nevertheless as soon as the war was over the Canadian project was directed entirely toward non-military objectives."[66]

This was false, as Pearson and several in the Liberal cabinet well knew, because Chalk River was then supplying plutonium for U.S. bombs, and Canada was then negotiating even bigger uranium export contracts with the U.S. military. Moreover, much of that ore was in Pearson's own electoral riding.

In 1953, the world's largest, richest uranium deposit was discovered in a 55-mile zig-zag formation in the hard-rock Algoma region between Sudbury and Sault Ste. Marie. The rich ore grade quickly underpinned the building of ten uranium mines, with all production contracted for U.S. and U.K bomb programs until 1962.

---

[66] Hansard, House of Commons debates; April 7, 1954

Pearson was delighted. At the official opening of the mammoth Denison mine, the largest in the western world, Pearson gushed that the Elliot Lake boom had been "fantastic, fabulous, frenzied and furious" and that the uranium would help ensure world peace.

"Our product stands between us and disaster," he declared.

The deposits in northern Saskatchewan and northern Ontario made uranium the leading Canadian mineral export in the late 1950's. They supported seventeen mines, employed nearly 20,000, and earned a cumulative $1.5 billion in revenues. The federally-owned Eldorado garnered glittering profits from its own mining and refining operations, and acted as sole broker for all private uranium ore sales to the U.S. and U.K.

In an extraordinary twist of political fate, by 1957 the Beaverlodge and Elliot Lake deposits were located in the ridings of Canada's two most prominent politicians. After a stunning federal election upset, the new Conservative Party prime minister was Saskatchewan's John Diefenbaker, and Lester Pearson became leader of a shell-shocked Liberal party now in opposition.

Both counted these exports of fissile material as a blessing, sales of bomb-grade plutonium from Chalk River to the U.S. military continued, and construction of an adjacent larger heavy-water reactor called NRU was completed in 1957. It cost $57 million, and featured a neutron density five times that of the NRX.

This meant it could produce ten times as much plutonium per year, virtually all of which was pre-contracted to the U.S. military. It had agreed to pay Canada about $5,000 per ounce, when the current price of gold was $35.[67] On this basis, Ottawa approved the NRU capital cost.[68]

Meanwhile, the isolated Sullivan mine near Val d'Or in northern Quebec became the major supplier of high-quality lithium for the U.S. hydrogen bomb program. It operated from 1946 to 1966.[69] The lithium was secretly shipped from the Quebec mine to a dedicated plant at the Oak Ridge complex in Tennessee, where it was processed for use in hydrogen bombs. Small amounts were used in the neutron "trigger" or detonator mechanism for fusion bombs, but most was mixed with deuterium (heavy water) to

---

[67] "Canada's Early Nuclear Policy", Buckley, pgs 77, 87
[68] "Canada's Nuclear Story"; Eggleston; pg 236
[69] This was purchased through the American Lithium Corporation.

comprise the thermonuclear fuel. As well, a heavy-water plant at Trail, B.C., called *Project 9* and financed by the U.S. military, produced 6 tonnes per year for export until 1955.

Finally, virtually all of the 70,000 tons of uranium shipped to the U.S. between 1945 and 1965 arrived as a natural uranium hexafluoride gas from the Eldorado refinery in Port Hope. The ratio of U_{235} to U_{238} was still 1:140, or seven parts per thousand. To make bomb-grade uranium, the Oak Ridge gaseous diffusion plant enriched the U_{235} isotopes to about 95 per cent concentration, then converted the gas into a metal for use in atomic and hydrogen bombs. Typically, each bomb required 20 kilograms of U_{235}, or less.

The Oak Ridge plant also distilled the U_{238} into a separate "depleted uranium" stream which was then converted to metal form. Some of this pure U_{238} was then sent to heavy-water reactors (based on the Canadian design) at the Savannah River military complex in South Carolina. There, it was shaped into special assemblies and irradiated in the reactor cores to become plutonium for bomb use. Or, the U_{238} was used in the inner casing of hydrogen bombs to boost the explosive output.

Did the Canadian government know, at the highest level, the precise use of these exports?

Without doubt. In August, 1953, federal Liberal cabinet member and 'minister for everything' C.D. Howe gladly accepted an invitation to tour the key U.S. bomb production plants. At the time, he sat on the federal cabinet Uranium sub-committee, along with the prime minister and Lester Pearson. It was considering an exclusive, 10-year contract for uranium sales to the USAEC.

Given a rare, high-level security clearance by his U.S. military hosts, Howe was briefed in detail about each step of the atomic and hydrogen bomb-making process, and personally inspected the Oak Ridge complex and Savannah River plutonium production reactors.[70]

He came home to Ottawa thrilled.

---

[70] ibid, pg 317

THE CRASH, THE CARTEL, AND THE COMEBACK

Canada's wild uranium joy-ride came to a sudden, near-fatal crash just after the stock markets closed on November 6, 1959. Ottawa and Washington tersely announced that the U.S. military would make no future uranium purchases beyond those under contract.

The news turned Elliot Lake and Uranium City into virtual ghost-towns. Some mines were padlocked within the month. Miners streamed south for new jobs like war-torn refugees, leaving forfeited mortgages and empty houses behind. After-tremors rocked the Toronto stock exchange. Recriminations flew in the House of Commons.

But all appeals fell on deaf ears. The reason was starkly simple: the U.S. military had almost 18,000 nuclear warheads - enough to destroy each Soviet city many times over. And it had perfected ways to recycle the original fissile bomb ingredients into new, more efficient warheads.

Then Britain made a similar announcement. Even the protests of prime minister Diefenbaker, and Liberal leader Lester Pearson, could not prevent the billion-dollar mineral from once again becoming mere pitch-blende worth pennies. These countries were then the only two customers for Canadian uranium, and both were now swamped with huge surpluses.

The uranium 'market' - founded solely on foreign government procurement and lavish Canadian government tax incentives - almost vanished overnight. The blow was softened slightly when the U.S. and U.K. agreed to stretch out the existing military contracts to 1965. That left a few large producers to cannibalize smaller ones, and federally-owned Eldorado with its own ore surplus, no refinery clients, and bleeding from the balance sheet.

Ottawa's solution was to single-handedly construct a new uranium 'market'. With still no domestic nuclear power plants in Canada, and only a trickle of foreign orders, a familiar white night came to their rescue: Lester Pearson.

In 1963, after a bitter election battle with Diefenbaker which featured Pearson stoutly *supporting* U.S. proposals to place nuclear-tipped Bomarc missiles in Canada, he emerged as prime minister. For obvious reasons, his new Liberal government agreed to pay $24 million to buy and stockpile uranium produced by the remaining Elliot Lake mines. It barely kept the mines operating, but it bought time for better days.[71]

---

[71] A small portion also supported a mine in Bancroft, Ontario.

Meanwhile, the largest company in Pearson's electoral riding, Denison, had been quietly negotiating a huge sale of uranium to the French government. In late 1964, it triumphantly announced an export contract worth $700 million. Only a promised approval from the Pearson cabinet stood in the way.

It never came. Instead, Pearson came under unexpected assault from Washington. When U.S. President Lyndon Johnson learned of the deal, he pulled out every diplomatic stop in Paris and Ottawa to block the deal - on non-proliferation grounds. France had exploded its first atomic bomb in 1960, and was developing an H-bomb. Johnson was adamant that the world's largest uranium reserve should not effectively fall into French hands.

Wilting, but desperate to salvage the mine in his riding, Pearson sent his external affairs minister, Paul Martin Sr. (who was then a director of Denison's parent company)[72] to Paris. His task was to press for a 'safeguards inspection' clause in the contract which would prevent the French from using the Canadian uranium in its weapons program.

French President Charles de Gaulle haughtily refused, and the $700 million deal died after several more diplomatic skirmishes. That left Denison, Elliot Lake, and the French in a fury, and Pearson humiliated. The debacle ended with Denison president Stephen Roman calling Pearson "a son of a bitch" to his face in the prime minister's office. Pearson later acidly observed that Roman was "fifty years behind the apes".[73]

When tempers cooled, a sweet-heart compensation package emerged. The Pearson cabinet agreed to buy and stockpile 15 million pounds of Denison uranium for $73 million. The price was just under $5 per pound, although an independent appraiser put Denison's production cost at $3.10. But this was only a down payment on future Ottawa largesse to support the uranium producers, and emerging CANDU reactor deals.

When Pierre Trudeau succeeded Pearson as prime minister in 1968, his cabinet approved yet another stockpiling program, this time under the aegis of a new federal corporation called Uranium Canada. The purpose was to buy and stockpile uranium from private Canadian producers, then barter it

---

[72] Roman Corporation was the parent company to Denison Mines, and apex of the corporate empire built by businessman Stephen Roman.
[73] "The Roman Empire" Paul McKay, pgs 106-110.

67

back when the world price rose. Or throw in low cost uranium as a sweetener tied to prospective foreign CANDU reactor sales being promoted by yet another federal agency, AECL.

In either case, Uranium Canada would buy millions of pounds of ore at the bottom of a market it expected to surge soon. The risk was minimal, because the Trudeau cabinet had plenty of inside knowledge on exactly how and when that would happen because Uranium Canada and Eldorado were secret members of an illegal, international cartel. The other conspirators included Denison, its Elliot Lake rival Rio Algom, Gulf Minerals Canada and its German partner Uranerz, uranium producers in Australia and South Africa, and the French government.

It lasted 60 months before documents leaked in Australia exposed the global bid-rigging scheme. It put an estimated $13 billion in cartel member coffers as prices artificially spiked 700 per cent. The cartel succeeded by setting internal quotas among its members, then rotating winning contrived 'bids' at ever escalating prices. The blind-sided victims were electric utilities in Europe, North America and Japan seeking fuel for nuclear power plants.[74]

The Canadian government was not a mere participant. Trudeau cabinet ministers and confidante's played key roles in creating the cartel, Eldorado and Uranium Canada helped rig the phoney bids, and federal officials served as the global cartel secretariat from government offices in Ottawa. The Canadian players won the biggest share of the illicit global sales proceeds.

When journalists learned that utilities in Ontario and the U.S. had been on the cartel hit list – a direct violation of anti-competition laws - the Trudeau cabinet passed draconian gag laws to keep details secret. They forbade any publication of cartel documents, reinforced by threats of $10,000 fines and 5-year jail terms.

It took years, but dozens of civil and criminal court cases inevitably forced many of the cartel members - including Denison, Rio Algom, and Gulf - into paying multi-million dollar settlements with those they had swindled. The Canadian players were also charged with criminal anti-combine conspiracy offenses by federal prosecutors.

---

[74] Ibid, chapter 8, "Cartel Blanche"

That compelled the Trudeau government to challenge its own justice department by claiming in the Supreme Court of Canada that Eldorado and Uranium Canada were not legally liable because they had obeyed superseding cabinet orders. The Supreme Court agreed. Five days later, on the pretext of preserving 'fairness', Trudeau's justice minister announced that the criminal charges facing the private Canadian cartel members would be dropped.

By then, the world price of uranium had dropped from a cartel high of $42 per pound back down to the pre-cartel price of about $8.

If justice did not catch up with the major Canadian uranium cartel players, the law of unintended consequences did.

The artificial spike in prices ignited an intense global prospecting search for new reserves, and that in turn confirmed that the world's largest, richest hidden deposits were in northern Saskatchewan. They would effectively put the Elliot Lake producers out of business.

But those new uranium titans would prove to have intimate links with the French atomic arms program, and Canadian exports of nominally 'peaceful' atoms would soon physically co-mingle in the French production complex used to make its *force de frappe*. That complex was created in the 1950's by Manhattan Project émigré scientists formerly based at Montreal's war-time labratory.

The French interest in Canadian uranium began with its failed bid to buy Denison's Elliot Lake mine in the mid-1960's. Despite world condemnation, France had continued to detonate atomic bombs in the Sahara desert, then hydrogen bombs in the south Pacific, to test its expanding arsenal. But France had almost no domestic uranium reserves to support its weapons program, or its ambitious nuclear power plant construction plans.

First thwarted by Washington, then stung by the cartel-induced climb in uranium prices in the early 1970's, the acutely vulnerable French government set out to solve both problems by locking down its own secure source. Then, as now, virtually all military and civilian nuclear facilities in France were state-owned, through a myriad of agencies and subsidiary corporations.

At the apex was (and is) a federal atomic energy commission, the CEA, through which the French presidency approved both its military and civilian nuclear programs, budgets, and operations. Key facilities were shared, and sensitive materials like plutonium were commonly co-produced, acquired, exchanged or recycled. There was no attempt to separate military or civilian atoms - even those imported.

Following the 1964 Denison contract debacle, France (through a state company called Cogema[75]) turned to northern Saskatchewan to supply uranium for its atomic arsenal, civilian reactors, and an extensive global client list of utilities operating nuclear power plants. Cogema acquired interests in a succession of rich ore deposits such as Cluff Lake, Key Lake and other "elephants" in the Athabasca basin.

By the late 1980's, this made Cogema the single largest uranium supplier in the western world. It was exporting some 7,000 tonnes per year from Canada, which would eventually be transmuted into more than 15,000 kilograms of plutonium annually.

Once this uranium was ship-bound for France, the CEA's state-sanctioned veil of secrecy kept virtually invisible exactly where those atoms would go. But gradually, through government leaks and journalistic reports, a clearer picture of the CEA operations - and its often sinister history - emerged.

The CEA was the essential legacy of the French heavy-water team once based in war-time Montreal - Bertrand Goldschmidt, Francis Perrin, and Lew Kowarski. They had all re-convened in Paris to build the French atomic programs from the ground up, with the highest support from its political and military leaders.

In October,1945, provisional French president Charles de Gaulle issued a directive to begin assembling the talent and materials to further military and commercial uses of atomic science. Frederic Joliot-Curie was designated to lead the CEA team, and its' first task was to build a heavy-water plutonium producing reactor, based on the NRX design, at a castle-fortress near Paris.

---

[75] Cogema was a subsidiary of the French federal CEA, as was Amok.

Joliet-Curie also pressed Ottawa for the return of the war-time heavy water originally smuggled from Norway. Documents confirm it was sent from Chalk River to Paris, via Britain, in 1948. France's first reactor, EL-1, went critical that December. One year later, the first milligrams of French plutonium were obtained by Bertrand Goldschmidt, using the solvent extraction process he had developed in Montreal.

Meanwhile, the French government had approved plans to build a second, larger heavy-water reactor at what would become the national atomic weapons lab in Saclay. When Joliet-Curie opposed this military trend in atomic research, he was stripped of his post. By 1951, Francis Perrin was the CEA president, Kowarski was chief designer of France's plutonium-production reactors, and Goldschmidt headed the team of chemists separating plutonium from used reactor fuel. In 1954, the French cabinet formally approved proceeding with an atomic bomb program.

This led to an industrial-scale plutonium production reactor (G-1) and extraction plant at Marcoule. It produced 12 kilograms of plutonium per year, which was extracted at an adjacent reprocessing plant built by the French industrial firm SGN. In 1959, two 200 Mw plutonium production reactors (G2, G3) were completed at Marcoule.

In February, 1960, France detonated its first plutonium bomb in the Algerian desert. It had a yield of 60-70 kilotons - three times the explosive force of the Nagasaki weapon.

During the next seven years, while the French plutonium stockpile grew, the CEA also built a mammoth gaseous diffusion uranium enrichment plant at Pierrelatte. Modelled on the U.S. plant at Oak Ridge, it could distil rare U_{235} isotopes to bomb-grade purity, and produce huge volumes of "depleted" U_{238} for use in plutonium production reactors, and hydrogen bombs.

In August, 1968, using plutonium, enriched uranium, and deuterium made within the CEA complex, France detonated a 2.6 megaton hydrogen bomb above an atoll in the south Pacific. It was ten times more powerful than the Nagasaki bomb, and left fallout so dirty the area was quarantined from humans for six years.

It was into this secret maze of military installations that the CEA subsidiary Cogema (which later morphed into Areva, the current French government conglomerate) began exporting ever escalating shipments of Saskatchewan uranium in the 1970's.

Since France resolutely refused to sign the 1970 U.N. Nuclear Non-Proliferation Treaty (NPT), none of these Canadian exports would be covered by atomic safeguards or subject to international inspections.

By the early 1960's an expanding circle of physicists and chemists knew that Canada's unique NRX and NRU reactors had high military value. Similar models were already producing plutonium for bomb programs in the U.S., Britain, Russia, and France.

For nations intent on building atomic weapons, a small heavy-water reactor was clearly the far faster, cheaper, and technologically accessible route than the gaseous diffusion plant needed to enrich the rare U_{235} isotope.

One of these countries was Israel. After its partition from Palestine in 1948 and the subsequent conflict with Egypt, its first leader David Ben-Gurion secretly began assembling scientific and intelligence teams to acquire the needed technology, knowledge and materials.

They were headed by Ernst Bergmann, a scientist who had served in the British defense department in the war, and Ben-Gurion's youthful but highly trusted protégé, Shimon Peres.[76] Few in Israel were told of the mission. A very small, university-scale research reactor was obtained from the U.S., but with stiff safeguard and inspection conditions Israel dared not defy.

Aware of Canadian negotiations to supply an NRX reactor to India, they turned their attention to the replica reactors then producing plutonium in France. Shimon Peres made personal contact with Bertrand Goldschmidt, the Jewish plutonium chemist who had worked in Montreal during the war, then married into the wealthy, well-connected Rothschild banking dynasty.

The Israeli's were quickly convinced that a heavy-water reactor was the best technical path to atomic weapons. That led to meetings with CEA director

---

[76] The principal sources for this section are: "The Samson Option" by veteran investigative journalist Seymour Hersh, and Michael Karpin's "The Bomb in the Basement". Both histories of the Israeli bomb program are consistent in all but the smallest of details with the memoirs of Bertrand Goldschmidt, and are extensively foot-noted.

Francis Perrin, who had published pre-war scientific papers on the complex calculations required to achieve a critical mass of uranium, and worked with the Montreal contingent of the Manhattan Project.

In the early 1950's, Peres was introduced to sympathetic French political leaders eager to cleanse the war-time Vichy regime's record of collaboration in the Holocaust. The Israeli's promised to lend the French CEA coveted computer talent to solve complex bomb design calculations, and in return were given unprecedented access to the weapons lab at Saclay, and the plutonium separation plant at Marcoule, for the next decade.

Then a tactical deal emerged. In exchange for $70 million in French-supplied military jets and ordnance, Israel agreed to launch a military strike against Egypt timed to coincide with pending 1956 French-British plans to seize the Suez Canal. [77] (Built by private French and British interests, the Suez had just been summarily expropriated by Egypt). Peres negotiated the terms with Ben-Gurion's approval.

The Israeli army did attack Egypt, but diplomatic threats from Russia and the U.S. persuaded Britain and then France to jettison their armed occupation of the Suez. That left Europe's most strategic shipping conduit in Egyptian hands, and Israel facing the wrath of Arab neighbour states for its provocative attack.

To atone, the French president later signed a secret agreement - drafted by Shimon Peres - to help build Israel a heavy-water reactor and an adjacent plutonium extraction plant. Peres had assured the French foreign minister they would be only used for peaceful purposes.[78] The latter was based on the process developed by Goldschmidt and built with French technicians from SGN, the company which had built the CEA plutonium separation plant at Marcoule.

Goldschmidt would later recall the Israeli nuclear appeal from Bergmann and Peres:

"They came to me and said they'd like to buy a heavy-water research reactor *similar to the one the Canadians were building in India*. They said that when the Americans realize we have the nuclear (weapons) capacity, they will give us the guarantee of survival".[79]

---

[77] "Bomb in the Basement", Karpin, pg 69
[78] ibid, pg 90
[79] "The Samson Option", pg 39. Emphasis added.

Anticipating potential objections from Washington, which was adamantly opposed to both France and Israel obtaining nuclear weapons, the two government's prepared to defend the deal on the pretext that it was no different than the recently announced unsafeguarded NRX reactor transfer from Canada to India.

But their secret held for another decade, in part by elaborate ruses to foil American inspectors, and outright lies to both Washington and the Israeli Knesset. To avoid raising alarms about the tell-tale scale of heavy water used at Dimona (which also furnished tritium and hydrogen-bomb fuel), Israel purchased it as 'research' material from suppliers in the U.S. and Norway.

Before his death, Bergmann conceded in an Israeli newspaper interview that civilian reactors like the NRX provided a useful camouflage to conceal military intent. "It's very important to understand that by developing atomic energy for peaceful purposes, you reach the nuclear (weapons) option. There are no two atomic energies."[80]

But in 1957 his country did not have millions to pay for the reactor and plutonium extraction plant. Also, Ben-Gurion and Shimon Peres wanted to keep the program secret even from the Knesset, the Israeli parliament.

Consequently, Ben-Gurion travelled to the U.S. to make a personal, private appeal to wealthy Jewish industrialists who had previously financed munitions and equipment purchases. They were known as the Sonneborn Institute, and included prominent Canadian families such as the Samuel Bronfmans and Louis Bloomfields of Montreal.[81] Their combined donations likely paid for the lion's share of the secret project.

Completed in mid-1968, both the reactor and plutonium separation plant were built far underground in the remote Negev desert to escape detection and possible destruction from Arab enemies. Using natural uranium and a heavy-water moderator, it soon began producing clandestine plutonium for the Israeli atomic arsenal, and eventually hydrogen bombs.[82] In 1970, Jericho rockets would allow compact warheads to strike targets as far away as the Soviet Union.

---

[80] Ibid, pg 26
[81] "The Bomb in the Basement"; Michael Karpin; pgs 136-38
[82] "The Samson Option"; pg 179

By then, only Shimon Peres remained alive among the original three atomic conspirators to savour this ephemeral hour of triumph. Soon, Iraq and Iran would be pursuing their own atomic weapons. To maintain Israel's advantage, Peres' next mission was to locate a place outside Israel to secretly test its untried nuclear bombs, and to acquire scarce uranium supplies.

First, in 1968 Israeli commandos covertly seized 200 tonnes of processed uranium (yellowcake) on board a cargo ship called the *Scheersberg A* during a night raid in the Mediterranean.[83] There was no on-board skirmish because the cargo - code-named 'plumbat'- had been pre-purchased by Israel through false front companies, and a compliant ship captain was warned in advance of the heist. Then, most brazenly of all, then Israeli defense minister Shimon Peres negotiated a secret deal in 1974 with John Vorster and P.W. Botha, then the prime minister and defense minister of the notorious apartheid government in South Africa. [84]

In exchange for purchasing South African uranium and a promised transfer of Jericho missile technology, Israel obtained that country's secret consent to jointly test atomic weapons above the Indian Ocean. That occurred in September,1979. It was simultaneously detected by the near-instantaneous double-flash captured by a U.S. VELA satellite orbiting above, and a radio-telecope signal picked up in Puerto Rico. Israeli and South African warships were observing nearby.

Later, a high-level South African naval official verified the Peres and Botha nuclear pact.[85] At least three successive 1979 Israeli atomic 'shots' likely took place. The fissile materials, deuterium and tritium in the Israeli bombs almost certainly came from the Dimona reactor, whose lineage could be traced directly back through France to the Chalk River NRX.

So could the carbon copies Canada had already delivered as 'peaceful' research reactors to India and its regional arch-rival, Pakistan.

---

[83] NYT Review of Books, May, 2004, letter by Victor Gilinsky, former U.S. Nuclear Regulatory Commissioner.
[84] Non-Proliferation Review; summer, 2004; "Israel and the South African Bomb"; Peter Liberman; pg 4
[85] The confirmation came from former South African navy commodore Dieter Felix Gerhardt.

Although few Canadians knew in the 1950's that the Chalk River reactors were prolific plutonium producers, one exception was a youthful theoretical physicist based in far-off India.

Homi Bhabha was nothing if not well-connected. He was born into a wealthy Parsi family, nephew to the patriarch of India's pre-eminent industrial dynasty, and political confidant of prime minister Jawaharlal Nehru by his early thirties. Equally important, he had earned his advanced physics degree at Cambridge University just as Chadwick and Cockcroft were making their famous atomic discoveries there.[86]

By all accounts, Bhahba was brilliant, urbane, charming, ambitious - and determined at all costs to bring India the nuclear bomb. Soon after Hiroshima, the Tata family provided him the finances to set up India's first atomic research centre, and Nehru appointed him leader of the country's atomic energy commission.

"Dr. Bhabha had in his mind from the very beginning that India should become a nuclear weapons state," his protégé and AEC successor P.K. Iyegar recalled. "His emphasis on self-reliance [multiple suppliers of nuclear technologies and fuels] is essentially due to the fact that he wanted India to be a nuclear weapons country."

Despite India's endemic poverty and depleted national treasury, for the next decade Bhabha's escalating federal funding requests met no resistance. This gave him the means, and prestige, to pursue atomic knowledge and bi-lateral technology transfers following the 1953 "Atoms for Peace" pledge by U.S. President Dwight Eisenhower.[87]

The U.S. program allowed, for the first time, the commercial export of civilian technology to developing countries. The Commonwealth countries, including Canada, followed this lead by fostering civilian nuclear technology transfers under the Colombo Plan.
Bhabha and his growing corps of scientific disciples took full advantage by obtaining research posts at western universities, flooding technical

---

[86] "India's Nuclear Bomb: The Impact on Global Proliferation"; George Percovitch; 1999
[87] At the time of Eisenhower's speech, the U.S. had detonated 42 atomic test bombs. "Bomb Scare"; pg23

conferences, and compiling what they had gleaned back in India. Bhabha himself circulated within the elite circles of western physicists, impressing all with his technical acumen and earnest assurances that India would pursue only the peaceful atom.

By 1955, he was in Chalk River at the invitation of its director W.B. Lewis, who had studied physics with Bhabha at the famous Cavendish laboratory in the 1930's.[88] The visit turned into an extended mission to study Canada's unique heavy-water reactors - and also proposed 'breeder' reactors which could allow India to take advantage of vast domestic reserves of the radioactive element thorium.

At the time, the 'breeder cycle' was passionately backed by Lewis, and many of Chalk River's leading scientists. It involved extracting plutonium from the spent fuel of a heavy-water reactor, then burning it in a second-stage reactor with thorium, which would be converted into the fissile element U_{233}. Then that U_{233} would be extracted from spent fuel and used in a third-stage thorium 'breeder' reactor to make even more fissile isotopes.

The premise was that since known world uranium reserves were finite, while global thorium deposits were essentially inexhaustible, the thorium 'breeder reactors' – powered by plutonium recycled from spent uranium reactor fuel - would inevitably become the dominant civilian power technology of the future. This, Bhabha assured Lewis, was his dream for India. A vast fleet of 'breeder' reactors would lift hundreds of millions from poverty, ensure resource independence, and put his country on the cutting edge of 21st Century science. Not incidentally, it might also be an alluring commercial opportunity for Canada.

The start would be giving India a plutonium-producing NRX at a loss-leader price, with generous credit terms. After that idea reached external affairs minister Lester Pearson, he lost no time obtaining federal cabinet approval to apply $14 million towards the project costs as part of Canada's Colombo Plan pledge. The optics, wrote Pearson, were excellent.[89] In July, 1955 Ottawa relayed the good news to New Delhi.

But Nehru's response one month later hinted that Bhabha's mission might have a military impetus. India now coveted not the NRX, but the larger NRU reactor, then almost completed at Chalk River, which could produce

---

[88] "Nucleus", Bothwell; pgs 350-370
[89] ibid, pg 353

ten times as much plutonium. (Neither of the reactors were designed to produce electric power).

As explanation, Nehru lamely insisted the NRX was unsuitable for its proposed Trombay site in India due to potential corrosion from ocean cooling water. Nehru did not explain why the NRX couldn't be re-located. He did offer to pay the extra costs for the larger reactor. Ottawa refused the 'trade up' offer, citing Canada's own lack of operating experience with the NRU, and its status as a dedicated plutonium producer, not a research reactor. Nehru eventually acceded, but resolutely resisted all suggestions that the NRX would be covered by safeguards.

Then in 1957 Bhabha announced that India would begin building its own plutonium extraction plant, based on the process the French chemist Bertrand Goldschmidt had developed. The obvious source of supply was the adjacent Canadian NRX - which could operate at the ocean site after all.

Despite this, brigades of Indian scientists continued to visit Chalk River to intensively study NRX reactor physics, heavy-water characteristics, plutonium extraction, and share in pioneering experiments with thorium and fissile U_{233}. Because all were embedded in the 'breeder reactor' concept, and Lewis shared a warm rapport with Bhabha, nothing was off limits.

Relations reached a high-water mark as the NRX replica at Trombay neared completion. By then, Indian technicians on the site outnumbered Canadians by 1,200 to 30. Bhabha insisted that half the fuel be made from Indian uranium, and deftly arranged to acquire 18.6 tonnes of heavy water from the U.S. government. Thus, the reactor was named CIRUS, an amalgam of the three nation partners.

It went critical in July, 1960. It could produce 8.6 kilograms of plutonium annually [90] - enough for one efficient warhead. Soon after, plans to send a much larger Canadian reactor to India were scoped out after Bhabha came to Ottawa and publicly mused that Russia was prepared to transfer unsafeguarded heavy-water reactor technology. And that the U.S. giant General Electric had its own rival reactors to vend to India.

This time, Bhabha wanted a 200 Mw CANDU power reactor, virtually identical to the proposed Douglas Point station in Ontario. Essentially scaled up from the NRX and NRU, the natural uranium, heavy-water reactor would produce large amounts of electric power - and some 133

---

[90] "Exporting Danger"; Ron Finch; pg 79

kilograms of plutonium each year for Bhabha's proposed 'breeder' reactors.[91]

But this time there was a prolonged contest of wills over safeguards. The new Kennedy administration was about to approve the General Electric reactor sale to India, with a sweetener of low-cost financing to parlay safeguards inspections and explicit bans on the diversion of plutonium. The U.S. deal included an $80 million loan at less than one per cent interest, to be repaid over 40 years in Indian rupees.

The U.S. safeguards measures were initially resisted by Bhabha and Nehru as examples of colonialism and 'atomic apartheid'. But they were under increasing pressure at home to finally build the grandiose nuclear power system they had promised, and the U.S. financial terms were too alluring to turn down. The deal was signed.

It was a double-edged precedent for Canada to match. Ottawa did gain the leverage to insist, like Washington, that the exported CANDU reactor (to be named RAPP-1) be subject to outside safeguards inspections, and that all the plutonium it produced be quarantined from military use. It took three years for Bhabha to grudgingly give up this ground. In the meantime, he played hard-ball on the RAPP-1 cost, negotiated an escalating percentage of Indian manufacturing content on future CANDU reactors, and won India the right to vend future knock-off models to other countries.

Bhabha, it seemed, was both a brilliant scientist and persuasive pirate. There was now little prospect that Ottawa might win commercial success with CANDU sales to India, and the CIRUS reactor, an NRX replica, remained exempt from safeguards.

Nevertheless, Ottawa reasoned, the new Indian deal would give the 200 Mw CANDU great marquee value for future sales to other developing nations. The reactor deal was finally signed in 1963, with provisions to build an accompanying heavy-water plant at Kota and sell India future reactors with increasingly less Canadian content. On the financing side, Ottawa agreed to provide a loan credit of up to $36 million - half the projected RAPP-1 cost.

It was a coup for Nehru and Bhabha, but neither would live to see the results. Nehru died of a heart attack in 1964, and Bhabha was killed in a 1966 plane crash. His sweeping dream of a prosperous India powered by

---

[91] ibid, pg 79

countless plutonium-thorium 'breeder' reactors vanished with him. But not his dream to build a bomb.

Because it was built and operated by Indian scientists, Homi Bhabha's plutonium extraction plant was not subject to any safeguards. The first spent fuel from the CIRUS reactor entered it on June 1, 1964, and the first bomb-grade grams of plutonium emerged on August 17.

Months later, India's northern boundary rival, Communist China, detonated the first of 45 atomic and hydrogen bombs at its Lop Nor desert site. Earlier, Moscow had supplied Beijing an NRX-style heavy water plutonium production reactor, uranium enrichment plant design, and lithium conversion technology.

Bhabha, in London in 1964 when the Chinese bomb was exploded, told reporters India could detonate its own within 18 months, and this impelled greater Indian political support for the undeclared weapons program. At the diplomatic level, Nehru and his successors aligned with Moscow in opposing U.N. adoption of proposed international safeguards rules. On the ground, Indian scientists continued assembling the technology and materials for a prospective nuclear arsenal.

In late 1964, CIA reports focussed on plutonium production at the unsafeguarded Canadian-supplied CIRUS reactor and adjacent plutonium extraction plant. One noted that the plutonium plant scale far exceeded that related to civilian use.[92] At the same time, Bhabha publicly declared that matching China's bomb would cost only $350,000.

If this pattern went undetected in Ottawa, it did not in Washington. The CIA had monitored India's nuclear status as early as 1958, and by October, 1965 predicted that the country might cloak a nuclear test under the guise of a 'peaceful nuclear explosive'.[93] A CIA memo dated that same month estimated that the Canadian reactor could produce 12 kilograms of

---

[92] U.S. Arms Control and Disarmament Agency memo; Indian Nuclear Problem; Oct 13, 1964
[93] "India's Nuclear Weapons Policy"; CIA SNIE 31-1-65, October, 1965

plutonium per year, and that India could "produce a dozen weapons in the 20 (kiloton) range by 1970." [94]

That chilling prospect was conveyed directly to Canadian prime minister Pierre Trudeau in January, 1971, by a top Pakistani scientist. Trudeau had just finished touring a CANDU reactor in Karachi, on a state visit to meet then Pakistani leader Ali Bhutto.

Trudeau also had a private lunch there with Dr. Ishrat Usmani, the former head of Pakistan's atomic energy commission. Usmani had resigned because Bhutto had ordered his scientists to use the CANDU for a plutonium bomb, and Trudeau was explicitly warned by Usmani that India might do the same.[95]

A 1972 analysis prepared for CIA director Richard Helms estimated that since 1963 "the CIRUS (NRX) reactor may have produced as much as 70 kilograms of plutonium, and 50-60 kilograms could already have been extracted at the nearby chemical separation plant and be available for use in nuclear devices". The Helms memo also concluded the two 200 Mw CANDU reactors then under construction at Rajthastan could each produce 160 kilograms of plutonium annually.[96]

By this time, the Canadian embassy in India was sending similar, albeit vague, warnings to Ottawa. And there was an obvious signal of India's intentions: it had refused to join 68 nations (including Canada) in signing the 1970 U.N. Nuclear Non-Proliferation Treaty (NPT) restricting the spread of atomic weapons. The Trudeau government sought assurances from India that plutonium from Canadian reactors would not be diverted for military purposes. Evasions prompted more appeals, which prompted more evasions. Yet construction on the CANDU projects did not stop.

The diplomatic dance ended abruptly on May 18, 1974. Acting on approval from India prime minister Indira Gandhi (but not her uninformed federal cabinet), Homi Bhabha's disciples detonated a plutonium bomb beneath the desert floor near the Pakistan border.

Code-named "Smiling Buddha", the 12-kiloton blast roughly equalled the Hiroshima bomb in explosive force, although most of the blast impact and

---

[94] The October 18, 1965 CIA memo was prepared by Donald F. Chamberlain, director of scientific intelligence.
[95] "The Islamic Bomb"; Weissman and Krosney; pg 133
[96] Internal memo to CIA director Richard Helms, Feb. 23, 1972

radiation was confined underground. The plutonium was forged inside the CIRUS heavy-water 'research' reactor. Now no one could deny that Canada's fingerprints were on a smoking gun.

At a press conference immediately following the 1974 blast, Indira Gandhi assured the world that the explosion was "nothing to get excited about" and merely a peaceful new tool for mega-scale excavations.

No one bought that evasion. Millions of jubilant Indians danced in the streets, thrilled to be a new atomic super-power. Newspapers were triumphant. Even Gandhi's parliamentary rivals, from communists to religious clerics, hailed the bomb builders as heroes. Her political status soared at home, at least for a few brief months until Indian courts convicted her of corruption, and she ordered 100,000 arrested under emergency power laws.[97]

But the 1975 bomb test brought India almost universal international condemnation, initially crippled its civil nuclear operations, and incited a perilous counter-move from its arch-rival, Pakistan. Ottawa and Washington cut off the supply of uranium, nuclear plants, and most related technical assistance to India. The two-country embargo would last for more than three decades - but it would not halt India's impetus to assemble refined atomic warheads, missile delivery systems, and hydrogen bombs.

Instead, India gradually built its nuclear arsenal production capacity using the beachhead technology 'gifted' by Canada and the U.S., an expanding fleet of cloned plants, and black-market components it clandestinely acquired from rogue suppliers.

These activities included obtaining uranium enrichment technology from France; heavy water supplies from China, Russia and Norway to operate the two Rajasthan CANDUs and CANDU clones; advanced computer technology from Norway; bomb-grade beryllium from Germany; and tritium and lithium purification technology of unknown origin.[98] Meanwhile, it continued to oppose international safeguards and inspections,

---

[97] "India's Nuclear Bomb", pg. 192. To forestall being stripped of power, in June, 1975 Indira Gandhi had opposition leaders arrested, suspended civil liberties, and eventually had more than 100,000 arrested.
[98] Wisconsin Project, India nuclear technology update (12 pages)

refused to sign nuclear test ban treaties, and developed warhead capable long-range missiles.

Eventually, India's nuclear production complex would comprise more than a dozen reactors, seven heavy water plants, enriched uranium facilities, several plutonium separation plants, and bomb design laboratories. The CIRUS and CANDU clones continued to produce more than 1,000 kilograms of unsafeguarded plutonium annually, and India even began exporting heavy water to supply a CANDU in South Korea.

In May, 1998 India detonated five nuclear bombs at its Pokhran desert test site, ranging in size from less than 1 kiloton to 45 kilotons. A senior government official, and atmospheric 'fission signature' tests, indicated that at least one was thermonuclear. In response, the Clinton administration imposed tough economic sanctions, and the World Bank suspended an $865 million loan.

Despite this censure, one month later Russia agreed to provide India with two large power reactors worth $2.6 billion. After September 11, 2001, citing India's promise to help fight terrorism, the U.S., Japan, Britain and finally Canada agreed to resume nuclear co-operation with India.

The principal condition was that India maintain a future 'parallel universe' of domestic civilian and military nuclear facilities. New reactors (including those of foreign suppliers) designated civilian would be subject to international safeguards inspections, along with the related fuel supplies and plutonium produced. Those India declared as military would be off-limits to inspections. Only a fence of intent would separate them.

Despite the May,1974 betrayal, and India's subsequent march to nuclear arsenal status, Ottawa took the new Indian assurances at face value. In September, 2005 Liberal external affairs minister Pierre Pettigrew publicly announced a new bilateral nuclear agreement with India allowing future sales of Canadian uranium and reactors.

It was as if the half-century of deception since Homi Bhabha's first arrival in Chalk River had never happened.

That same month, Liberal deputy prime minister Anne McLellan arrived in Pakistan, leading a trade mission to sell Canadian uranium and reactors.

On her September, 2005 schedule was a personal meeting with Pakistan's leader, General Pervez Musharraf, to discuss how Canada might assist in his country's plan to build and fuel as many as a dozen new nuclear power reactors. Billions worth of possible export orders were at play. Afterward, both McLellan and Musharraf were careful to publicly stress that while Canada and Pakistan opposed the proliferation of atomic weapons, all nations had sovereign rights to pursue peaceful nuclear technology.

It was a moment of brazen duplicity.

Pakistan was then the word's newest - and most notorious - nuclear weapons proliferator. Musharraf, a former army chief of staff who had seized power in a 1999 coup, fully supported the weapons program. He had previously declared as a national hero Abdul Qadeer Khan, the Pakistani scientist who was the mastermind of a global nuclear espionage ring.

By then the world knew that Khan's covert network had operated for decades, buying and trading sensitive nuclear technologies for not only Pakistan, but rogue states like Libya, North Korea, and Iran. In 2004, Khan had publicly confessed to his crimes, yet been immediately pardoned by Musharraf. At the time of McLellan's visit he was under a nominal house arrest order, shielding him from foreign intelligence probes, and questions from international safeguard inspectors Khan had eluded for decades.

There was no possibility that McLellan, the Canadian deputy prime minister, had not been briefed by her embassy staff about Pakistan's nuclear weapons status, the close bond between Musharraf and Khan, or the fact that decades earlier Canada had supplied Pakistan a heavy-water CANDU.

Called KANUPP, it was a smaller version of those supplied to India, yet still capable of producing 82 kilograms of plutonium annually.[99] With future CANDU orders now at risk, McLellan apparently thought it best to let the world assume Khan's bomb team had succeeded without any help from Canada.

---

[99] "Exporting Danger"; Ron Finch; 1986; pg 80

84

Yet there was a prominent public photograph of A.Q. Khan, and Canadian-trained weapons specialist Ishfaq Ahmad triumphantly posing together at the 1998 Pakistani atomic blasts.[100] In fact, Canada's reactor had been targeted for covert plutonium diversion twenty-five years earlier.

Pakistan's atomic bomb program began on January 20, 1972 at a secret summit convened at a remote colonial mansion by Ali Bhutto, the new leader of a nation reeling from traumatic events. After a bitter civil war, its former eastern half had separated into independent Bangladesh. To rub salt into the wound, India had sided with Bangladesh and routed the Pakistani forces during the conflict.

Bhutto's summit was convened in a spirit of humiliation and raw revenge. Earlier, as Pakistan's foreign minister, he had publicly warned: "If India builds the bomb we will eat grass, or leaves, or even grow hungry. But we will get one of our own."

Now Bhutto meant to keep that vow. Among the elite scientists gathered at the retreat near the historic city of Muran were future Nobel laureate Abdus Salam, Ishmat Usmani, the head of Pakistan's atomic energy commission (PAEC), and physicist Munir Ahmed Khan.

Salam and Usmani refused to endorse Bhutto's bomb program. Salam left for Italy, and Usmani took up a post with the U.N. in New York. One year earlier, Usmani had personally warned Canadian prime minister Pierre Trudeau in Karachi about the latent peril of plutonium diversion from CANDU reactors.

Munir Khan assured Bhutto a bomb could be built. It was he who stepped into the scientific leadership vacuum as new chairman of the PAEC, which he would use as a front to covertly build Pakistan's bomb.[101] The choice was clever, and pre-ordained.

Munir Khan had secretly been pressing Pakistani leaders to begin a bomb program since the 1960's, even while he held a senior position at the international agency meant to *prevent* proliferation. As head of reactor

---

[100]   At the time, the photo was posted on an official Pakistani defense journal website
[101]   "The Islamic Bomb" pgs 42-48

engineering at the International Atomic Energy Agency (IAEA), Munir Khan had convened several conferences on civilian heavy-water reactor operations and plutonium separation.

Now he was ready to use his IAEA credentials, and his new PAEC post, to help camouflage the Pakistani weapons effort. Among his first conscriptees would be Ishfaq Ahmad, who had earned his advanced physics degrees at universities in Montreal and Ottawa.

Both Khan and Amhad had been among 13,000 science students from developing nations trained in 'atoms for peace' programs at U.S., Canadian and European universities. Ahmad would later conduct 'cold testing' of Pakistan's first bombs in 1983, assume the PAEC chair post after Munir Khan's death in 1991, and personally direct the inaugural 1998 Pakistani bomb tests.

From the beginning, aided by Libyan and Saudi petro-dollars, the Pakistani scientists pursued a two-track strategy to assemble the future atomic arsenal. While A.Q. Khan began covertly assembling uranium enrichment equipment, the Canadian-supplied 137 Mw KANUPP power reactor was central to the plutonium path. Munir Khan knew it well. It was he who had negotiated the deal with Ottawa, which featured a $51 million loan, at zero interest, repayable over fifty years.[102] The reactor went critical in August, 1971.

The CANDU reactors, including KANUPP, had unique features suitable for covert plutonium production. First, they could make the fissile material while producing electric power - and thus provide a civilian camouflage. Second, the plutonium production rate was superior due to its high neutron flux. Third, the CANDU could be constantly re-fueled without a shutdown. Finally, the plutonium 'burnup' rate could be covertly adjusted to maximize bomb-grade quality.[103]

But there were still two obstacles: Pakistan then had no plutonium separation plant, and the KANUPP reactor was subject to limited safeguard inspections as a condition of the generous Canadian financing.

---

[102] "Canada and the Nuclear Arms Race", Regehr, Rosenblum, Edwards; Chapter 6, pg 128; David Martin;   "Exporting Disaster"
[103] One way to achieve this was to put undeclared depleted uranium (pure U 238) slugs into some fuel channels inside the reactor. This would produce more plutonium. They could be removed and replaced with regular fuel bundles, and the diversion would be virtually impossible to detect.

Munir Khan and his team solved the first problem by turning to an old master of plutonium extraction with special knowledge of the Canadian technology - Bertrand Goldschmidt of France. It was Goldschmidt who had conceived the solvent separation technique in war-time Montreal, used it to build France's first bombs, and passed on the secrets to Israel for use at the Dimona heavy water reactor.

Now Goldschmidt was a senior figure in France's CEA, and its point man for pending sales of French plutonium reprocessing plants to countries like Pakistan, India, South Korea, Taiwan and Iraq. A pilot plant was built to separate the KANUPP spent fuel. Then in 1973 a French-Pakistan contract was signed for a 100-tonne per year plutonium separation plant, called Chashma, to be built by the CEA affiliate, SGN.

The Chashma plant was scaled to give the Bhutto government 200 kilograms of plutonium each year, enough for an escalating arsenal. Once Pakistan was ready to build a bomb, plutonium from the accumulated spent fuel at KANUPP could be used despite belated Canadian protests.

When news of the deal leaked out, alarm bells went off in Washington and New Delhi, but Ottawa's response remained mute. That changed after May, 1974 when India detonated its first bomb using plutonium from the CIRUS reactor. Now Ottawa faced a diplomatically damaging repeat performance from India's bitter regional rival, Pakistan.

But neither Bhutto nor France would back down from their deal. In October, 1974, detailed blueprints and plant layouts for the Chashma project were delivered by SGN, with Goldschmidt's stamp of approval.

The pending Pakistani plutonium re-processing plant construction, and the Indian atomic bomb test, impelled Washington to action. After the Oak Ridge nuclear laboratory concluded that a small, crude plutonium reprocessing plant could be covertly built in two years, for tens of millions, and separate enough reactor-grade plutonium for several weapons annually, the Carter administration took a tough stance against plutonium extraction from civilian spent fuel at home and abroad.[104]

---

[104] "A Preliminary Analysis of the ORNL Memorandum on a Crude Nuclear Fuel Reprocessing Plant"; Congressional Research Service; Warren H. Donnelly; November, 1977; also "Energy/War" Lovins, pg 21

The U.S. Congress passed a strict law to prevent sensitive nuclear exports, and Washington pressed for the adoption of an international "trigger list" of atomic components forbidden for global commerce. This put the U.S. and France on a diplomatic collision course over the Pakistani plutonium plant, and Canada awaiting the outcome with held breath. With Pakistan still refusing to sign the NPT or upgrade safeguards on KANUPP, Ottawa imposed an embargo on future nuclear assistance in January, 1977.

But the Canadian reactor kept running, and by the end of the year was in the hands of a ruthless military dictator, General Zia ul Haq. He had deposed Ali Bhutto in a coup, and would have him executed in 1979. Zia pressed the French to complete the Chashma plutonium separation plant, and now considered the KANUPP plutonium to have been abandoned by Canada.

International inspectors were denied requests to put cameras, counters and seals inside the Canadian reactor, and inspections were delayed long enough to speed up plutonium production. In November, 1981 the IAEA formally reported it could give no assurance plutonium had not been diverted at KANUPP.[105]

Meanwhile, A.Q. Khan's espionage network had been stealing or purchasing, piece by piece, classified blueprints and thousands of precision parts needed to build the Kahuta U_{235} enrichment plant in Pakistan. They came from the Netherlands, Germany, England, Italy, Japan, China, Malaysia, the U.S. and Canada. He obtained a bomb blueprint from China, traded secrets to North Korea in exchange for rocket technology transfers, and sold spare or duplicated U_{235} enrichment plant parts to Iran and Libya.

He also clashed with Munir Khan, and both became rivals in a race to furnish the bomb ingredients first. Each was given a prestigious laboratory, staff, money and trade conduits through Pakistani embassy's abroad. Their mediator, and the overall director of the Pakistani weapons program, became the Canadian-trained physicist, Ishfaq Ahmad.

Eventually, the French withdrew financing and technical support for the large Chashma plutonium separation plant, and Pakistan adapted by enlarging its plutonium separation labs. Later, it built a heavy-water plutonium production reactor at Khushab, a heavy water plant, and a tritium extraction plant.

---

[105] "The First Nuclear World War"; Lovins, Lovins, O'Heffernan; William Morrow; 1983; page 126

88

All this was in place when Canada's Anne McLellan met General Musharraf in Pakistan in 2005. As of that date, Pakistan had finally mastered both production routes to the atomic bomb, the means to add at least a dozen new uranium and plutonium weapons to its arsenal each year, and missile technology which could strike far into India.

Nevertheless, she told the military strongman, Pakistan was a promising place for Canada to do more nuclear business.

By then, Ottawa had plenty of practice in atomic commerce with depraved dictators.

One of the most brutal was Argentine general Jorge Videla, who led a military junta which overthrew the Isabel Peron government in March, 1976. It ended in 1983, leaving some 30,000 dead or 'disappeared' from a domestic 'Dirty War', and the nation disgraced for provoking - and losing - the Falklands War with Britain. General Videla was later convicted of multiple murders, and for authorizing a black-market involving infants born to mothers imprisoned during the junta. His lesser crimes included the suspension of courts and civil liberties, repressing dissent, banishing trade unions, and driving the country deep into debt.

It was to this junta that Ottawa delivered a 600 Mw reactor capable of producing 413 kilograms[106] of plutonium annually - *after* India had exploded its test bomb using the much smaller CIRUS reactor. It also guaranteed a five-year supply of uranium, and reactor fuel fabrication services.[107]

The bid to sell the CANDU to Argentina was approved by the Trudeau cabinet in May, 1972, and then co-submitted with an Italian partner [108] to the military regime of General Alejandro Lanusse. It was accepted before the Peron government came to power. Protracted negotiations ended in December, 1973, and the contract terms came into force in April, 1974.[109]

---

[106] "Exporting Danger"; pg 90
[107] Letter from federal energy minister Marc Lalonde to Saskatchewan MLA Peter Prebble, August 7, 1981.
[108] Italiapianti
[109] "Exporting Danger"; Finch; pg 53

89

Weeks later, India detonated its first atomic test. That swung a spotlight onto the Canada-Argentina reactor deal, because it had refused to sign both the U.N Non-Proliferation Treaty, and a parallel treaty for Latin America countries. But Argentina had agreed to limited safeguards inspections on the Canadian reactor, so the preliminary construction was approved.

Then a scandal broke in Ottawa over the contract terms. The crown corporation Atomic Energy of Canada Ltd. (AECL) was discovered to have paid $2.4 million in bribes (via its Italian partner) to secure the deal. Worse, it was revealed that Ottawa was financing $155 million of the $420 million projected cost with a 25-year, low interest loan. Worse still, the contract failed to protect AECL against soaring inflation, since Canada was to be repaid in highly de-valued Argentine currency.

When the Videla junta seized power in 1976, the Canadian government was facing a $200 million loss on the CANDU sale. AECL begged to re-negotiate, and eventually settled for a $130 million loss.

But by then the Videla regime was killing, kidnapping and dismissing many of Argentina's leading physicists for opposing imported technology, and this delayed the CANDU construction. Alarms mounted in Washington and Ottawa after it was revealed that the Argentine nuclear program, now under Navy control, also involved a unsafeguarded plutonium separation plant at Ezeiza capable of separating 10-20 kilograms per year, and a uranium enrichment lab at Pilcanyeu.[110]

At the time, the Trudeau cabinet was explicitly warned of this prospect, as a leaked summary attests:

"Argentina continues to show no inclination to accept Canadian [safeguards] requirements. In fact, Admiral Madero has in recent statements been unequivocal in rejecting NPT and full-scope safeguards, while re-affirming his country's desire to retain a nuclear explosives option. Argentina is well on the way to developing an indigenous fuel cycle that is completely free of safeguards."[111]

These proliferation dangers, and the Videla junta's lurid record of human rights abuses, prompted the May, 1982 blockade of 3,000 uranium fuel

---

[110] "Tracking Nuclear Proliferation"; 1998, Carnegie Endowment research paper; Jones, MacDonough et al
[111] "Canada and the Nuclear Arms Race" pg 150, citing a memo leaked to the Ottawa Citizen.

bundles bound for Argentina by union longshoreman in New Brunswick. They were produced from Saskatchewan uranium by the federal crown company Eldorado Nuclear. To circumvent the harbour blockade, the Trudeau government had the uranium flown to Buenos Aires from Montreal.

Capable of producing enough plutonium for 50 warheads per year, the CANDU reactor at Embalse, Argentina was completed in 1983, the same year the brutal junta rule ended. A 1979 AECL bid to sell a duplicate CANDU and NRX reactor to the regime failed.

Fortunately, later civilian governments would dismantle the clandestine Argentine plutonium and enrichment plants, sign the NPT, and put General Videla on trial for his many crimes. But enough plutonium for an estimated 1,200 bombs remains in the CANDU spent fuel there.

While the Trudeau cabinet was considering approval of the CANDU sale to the Videla junta, parallel negotiations were taking place with the dictator of South Korea, Park Chung-Hee.

Park had seized power in 1961, and he maintained a rigid, repressive regime until his assassination in 1979. Seen as a bulwark against Communist expansion from North Korea and China, South Korea was heavily subsidized by U.S. spending on its forward military bases there, and by concessionary federal export loans underwriting power reactor sales by U.S.-based Westinghouse.

Inexplicably, the Park regime indicated in early 1973 that it would look favourably on a bid by AECL to provide a 600 Mw replica of the Argentina CANDU reactor. At the time, Westinghouse was offering two more reactors, at cut-throat costs. If Canada could win a contract, it would be a competitive coup.

The proposed deal went before the Trudeau cabinet in June, 1973, and approval was given to proceed with more detailed contract terms. Negotiations were delayed after the Indian atomic bomb test in 1974, but resumed after South Korea reluctantly signed the NPT in 1975. At the time, the U.S. had suspended the Westinghouse reactor loans until the Park dictatorship acceded to the NPT and safeguards inspections.

The $576 million CANDU sale was finalized in January, 1976. Then U.S. intelligence wiretaps of Park's presidential palace uncovered discussions about a covert plutonium separation lab in South Korea,[112] and Washington learned that the Park regime was negotiating to buy a large plutonium reprocessing plant from France.

Spear-heading that sale was Bertrand Goldschmidt, the French chemist who had worked in war-time Montreal on plutonium separation. At the same time, Goldschmidt was also negotiating the sale of a large plutonium separation plant (a replica of that proposed to Pakistan) to the military regime in Taiwan - to which Canada had just sold an NRX reactor.[113] It was closed after a U.S. inspection team concluded the NRX was being used to covertly make plutonium.[114]

This put the proposed CANDU sale to South Korea - which could produce enough plutonium for 50 warheads per year - in the middle of a diplomatic confrontation between the U.S., South Korea, and France. The Carter administration could not stop the Canadian reactor sale, but it was adamant that Park would get no access to plutonium separation technology. Eventually, the French sale was aborted, and the plutonium lab dismantled.

But controversy did not end there. As details about the bribes and losses on the Argentina CANDU contract emerged, Parliamentary opposition members and the press turned a spotlight on the South Korea deal. Despite months of stone-walling from the Trudeau cabinet, it was discovered that the Wolsung deal had been greased with a $20 million 'agents fee' AECL paid to a mysterious Israeli broker, Shaul Eisenberg, though a myriad of corporate shells and addresses.[115]

It was also revealed that the federal Export Development Corporation (EDC), under authorization from the Trudeau government, was financing the CANDU sale to South Korea with a concessionary long-term loan of $430 million. [116]

---

[112] "The Islamic Bomb"; pg 151
[113] ibid, pg 152-153. This proposed deal was also squelched after intense opposition from the Carter administration.
[114] The team was led by proliferation expert Armando Travelli. His mission was kept secret to avoid embarrassment to Canada. Chicago Tribune; Sam Roe; Jan. 28, 2007
[115] This was later 'reduced' to $18.5 million, on the understanding Eisenberg could recoup his loss on future CANDU sales.
[116] "Exporting Disaster", pg 32

This effectively meant that Ottawa would guarantee payments to the Canadian and British component suppliers for their work on the Wolsung reactor, then recover those payments through the loan agreement with South Korea over a decade or more. It was a sweet deal for the CANDU contractors, and the Park regime.

But it put a huge risk on the balance sheet of the federal government,[117] and left AECL waiting for more lucrative reactor sales to South Korea. By then, Park had been replaced by an equally repressive president, Chun Doo Hwan, who closed newspapers, curtailed freedom of speech and assembly, and ordered federal troops to crush public demonstrations. In May, 1982, 2,000 civilians were killed and 10,000 were injured by Hwan troops during anti-government protests.

Despite this, the Saskatchewan government sought uranium sales to the South Korean regime, and in 1983 even offered to sell it $2.7 million shares of provincially co-owned uranium properties. Eventually, contracts for three more CANDU reactors would be signed and construction would proceed in the 1990's, but with increasingly less Canadian content. The proliferation risk faded from view until 2003, when international safeguards inspectors challenged the South Korean government - then confronting a deranged dictator in North Korea - about clandestine plutonium separation and uranium enrichment work. After repeated evasions, deliberate ruses, and blocked inspections, Seoul confirmed that the plutonium work had been done in 1982, and U_{235} enriched to 77 per cent in 2000, using advanced laser technology.[118]

Once again, safeguards promises proved to be a hoax, leaving Ottawa exposed by a reversal of declared intentions. As with the India debacle, AECL would never get beyond loss-leader pricing and barter away the rights to clone future CANDUs. Yet it consigned to South Korea - a nation facing a hostile, nuclear-armed northern neighbour - Canadian designed reactors making enough plutonium to construct more than 100 warheads each year for decades.

---

[117] The Canadian federal government is the guarantor of EDC debt.
[118] Washington Post, Dafna Linzer; Sept 12, 2004

When Romanian dictator Nicholi Ceausescu was executed by a military firing squad in December, 1989, he left behind raging mobs, a sumptuous palace, Swiss bank accounts, a wrecked economy, thousands killed by ruthless security police and civil unrest, slave labor camps, and tens of thousands of orphaned children living in appalling conditions.

His neo-Stalinist legacy also included a covert lab separating plutonium and high-enriched uranium for a nascent bomb project,[119] and a signed contract to purchase a CANDU power reactor capable of producing more than 400 kilograms of plutonium annually.

As with the Argentina and South Korea deals, serious negotiations with the Romanian dictator began under the Trudeau government in the mid-1970's. In this case, obtaining a safeguards agreement was not an obstacle, since Romania had signed the NPT and agreed to allow future reactor inspections.

What was immediately problematic was money. Romania claimed to have none, and bargained hard to win a licencing agreement instead of an outright purchase of the 600 Mw CANDU.[120] This meant Romania would pay $5 million to obtain all the detailed blueprints for a first reactor, then as low as $2 million for future units. In related contracts, Canadian content would also diminish with each successive reactor built.

The negotiations between AECL and the Romanian state trading company Romanergo were kept confidential until Trudeau cabinet approval was obtained. In November, 1978, the federal Export Development Corporation publicly disclosed that it was arranging a $1 billion line of credit to support the sale of four CANDUs to Romania. A consortium of banks would provide $320 million of that, secured by EDC guarantees. The following month, Ottawa gave the deal final approval.

It was not disclosed that the $1 billion in EDC financing only covered the *first* CANDU, and that the Canadian content on that reactor would be worth only $100 million of the $800 million capital cost.[121] So the Romanian regime was effectively paid to obtain the CANDU blueprints, and obliged only to ensure minimal Canadian content on future reactors if they were built. But worse was to come. After the initial $320 million had

---

[119] This was formally reported to the IAEA by the Romanian government in 1992.
[120] Later boosted to 700 Mw.
[121] "Exporting Danger" ps 141-144

94

been spent, Romania claimed it had no foreign currency with which to repay the EDC-backed loans. It wanted to 'contra-trade' Romanian tractors, steel and strawberries for an equivalent value in CANDU components and engineering services.

Canada refused. Ceausescu himself came to Ottawa to make the case, then belatedly tried to sweeten his 'contra-trade' offer by agreeing to build a second CANDU. It was declined. Ottawa wanted no part of a deal which would force Canadian manufacturers to compete with dumped Romanian goods inside their own country.

In June, 1982, the EDC halted loan payments to Romania. Ceausescu responded by negotiating a rival reactor deal with Russia, and announcing that unpaid foreign debts exceeding $1 billion would not be repaid. Now Canada was forced to choose between walking away from a $320 million loss, or upping the ante.

Even though Romania's foreign debt then exceeded $11 billion, Ottawa upped the ante. In late 1983, the EDC proposed a $2 billion line of credit to cover the cost of building two CANDUs in Romania. Far from grateful, the increasingly tyrannical Ceausescu demanded that the 'contra-trade' repayments be expanded to include consumer goods like textiles, shoes and wine.

Although details remain murky, the dictator apparently called Ottawa's bluff and won his 'contra-trade' terms. Construction of the first CANDU at Cernavoda was resumed, with only a skeleton staff of Canadian engineers on site. The project was largely built by brigades of army 'black battalions' living in squalid barracks and given meagre rations, or conscripted slave labourers.[122]

Construction stopped during the 1989 national uprising against Ceausescu, and immediately following his execution. It resumed in 1991 after AECL and an Italian partner took over project management and most financing. By 1995, the cost for the first reactor had climbed to $2.2 billion. It was commissioned in 1996 - two decades after the initial contracts were signed. A second 700 Mw CANDU clone began operation at Cernovada in 2006.

The two reactors can each produce more than 400 kilograms of plutonium annually.

---

[122] "Exporting Danger" pg 28

DOWN AND DIRTY WITH THE
BUTCHER OF BEIJING

In November, 1994 Prime Minister Jean Chretien and Communist leader Li Peng of China jointly signed a landmark nuclear co-operation agreement. It came with the solemn caveat that future transfers of CANDU nuclear technology and uranium would be confined to civilian uses only.

The agreement was controversial. China was defying a moratorium on nuclear bomb testing then being honoured by the U.S., Britain, Russia and France. It had many nuclear facilities exempt from proliferation safeguards and inspections (including heavy-water reactors which had produced 2.8 tonnes of surplus weapons-grade plutonium)[123] and an arsenal which included atomic and hydrogen bombs.

The Chinese military regime was also selling, through the A.Q. Khan espionage network, nuclear bomb designs and components to Pakistan, as well as long-range missile technology. This had prompted the U.S. to formally halt all nuclear reactor sales to China and Pakistan.

Finally, Li Peng was infamous as the "Butcher of Beijing" for his role in authorizing the 1989 Tiananmen Square massacre of unarmed students.

But Ottawa was prepared to ignore all these troubling issues if China would allow site-specific outside inspections of any future CANDU projects. When Li Ping gave this assurance, Jean Chretien authorized Atomic Energy of Canada Ltd. (AECL) to proceed with negotiations on a two-reactor deal.

That's when contract talks got down and dirty.

China was adamant on three points: Canada had to loan China $4 billion (converted to U.S. dollars) to buy the reactors; the money had to be routed through a Chinese state bank which would repay the loan over decades; and the two-reactor deal must be sealed by November, 1996.[124]

For AECL and Canadian private sector nuclear suppliers, the terms and timetable were brutal. There was faint hope Jean Chretien's Liberal cabinet

---

[123] "Plutonium"; Bernstein; pg 169

[124] This chapter is based on an Ottawa Citizen series of stories by the author, published in June, 1998. They were based on primary federal government documents cited by department, agency or cabinet office.

96

would immediately approve the $4-billion loan needed to keep the CANDU-China project all-Canadian -- on top of cumulative federal nuclear subsidies of some $20 billion since the 1950s.

There was also no hope AECL and its allies could obtain the $4 billion from commercial banks. By the first week of January, 1995, AECL president Reid Morden had already made his funding pitch at an Ottawa meeting attended by deputy or associate deputy ministers of Finance, Natural Resources and International Trade. The latter, Allen Kirkpatrick, would soon become AECL's vice-president of marketing and sales.

The strongest advocates within the federal bureaucracy were in the nuclear division at Natural Resources Canada, for which Alberta Liberal MP Anne McLellan was cabinet minister. They promised a budget by the end of January, a position paper, and briefing notes for other Chretien cabinet ministers. But the initial response was ominous: $4 billion was beyond the budgetary pale.

In late January, 1995, AECL's China specialist Herman Chang sent a memo to Natural Resources with a heavy hint that unless the cabinet approved a loan of at least $2.4 billion, on terms ``less expensive than commercial financing,'' the China sale - and Canadian equipment orders for Quebec sub-contractors - might be lost. That message was not lost on the prime minister's office.

Speaking at a Montreal conference on trade with China weeks later, Chretien assured the business audience: ``When the CANDU sale goes ahead, companies in Quebec will earn hundreds of millions of dollars as suppliers. That is how Team Canada works. That is how it works for every region of Canada.''

The private nuclear supply companies Chretien was enticing in his flag-waving speech took him at his word. The following week, the prime minister, eight cabinet ministers and two key deputy ministers received letters pressing for full federal financing of the reactor sale to China.

``It is the understanding of the companies involved in this important sale that the Chinese require an indication that adequate financing will be available to cover 100 per cent of the project costs,'' wrote Alex Taylor, president of Agra Industries Ltd. ``I understand the interdepartmental committee reviewing the government's position will be recommending less than full government of Canada financing for the Canadian supply portion of the sale.''

By early March, 1995, AECL and its allies were pressing for face-to-face meetings with top officials for Finance, International Trade, Natural Resources and the Export Development Corporation. With the Chinese contending they were also courting French and U.S. reactor suppliers AECL had to have answers. Fast.

``Due to the urgency of presenting a Canadian financing proposal to the Chinese, we request that the meeting occur in the week of March 13, with a view to getting Cabinet approval for the financing proposal by the end of the month," said a memo signed by AECL and four major private-sector suppliers.

The memo stopped just short of an ultimatum. Documents show it triggered a new round of high-level sessions at the deputy minister level, including working weekends. It also brought prime minister Chretien's chief Privy Council advisers into the loop, and prompted a spate of Foreign Affairs cables between Ottawa and the Canadian embassy in Beijing.

It also sparked an analysis of the proposed deal by senior advisers to finance minister Paul Martin. A March 20, 1995 report warned that the credit risk premium on the loan could be as high as 25 per cent, that the Chinese state bank designated to receive the money had no credit rating, and that the federal government could face major currency exchange losses.

That ominous report, reminiscent of previous CANDU deals with Argentina, South Korea, and Romania gone bad, was ignored. One week later - without finished text formatting or a French translation - the AECL/China loan proposal was signed by Natural Resources Minister Anne McLellan and put in the queue for cabinet approval.

Pushback from AECL, private Canadian nuclear suppliers, and supportive bureaucrats seemed to be working. The China CANDU deal was back on track.

On March 31, McLellan's deputy minister, Jean McCloskey, wrote China's chief nuclear negotiator. Her letter opened by saying:

``The Canadian government is in the final stages of approving a financing offer for the proposed CANDU project to be built at the Qinshan site in China. As I am sure you are aware, the government of Canada has recently taken strong action to reduce our financial deficit, including making large reductions to budgets of government departments. The fact that it will, at

98

this difficult time, commit to an offer of a substantial financing package indicates the importance that nuclear trade with China represents in our priorities, and particularly those of our prime minister."

The trouble was: nobody outside a select few in the Chretien inner circle knew then what those ``substantial financing'' numbers were. The Canadian public still doesn't.

The Liberal cabinet eventually approved a $1.5-billion loan guarantee for the AECL/China deal. That represented the principal only. As the Finance memo of March 20 noted, the cumulative cost of the deal to federal taxpayers would depend on the provision for the credit risk, the loan interest rate, and the potential losses on currency exchanges. On a loan payback projected at 22 years, these additional costs could be hundreds of millions of dollars.

There was no doubt that the federal Treasury - not AECL - would be the ultimate guarantor of the $1.5-billion loan. A Finance memo noted: ``In the event of a default by China, Canada will be forced to purchase U.S. dollars in the market at an uncertain exchange rate to pay bondholders.''

But the $1.5-billion loan commitment wasn't enough for the Chinese. They wanted a bigger loan, in U.S. dollars, at a cheaper interest rate. And the CANDU was too expensive. France, they told AECL, could do much better.

That response caused near-panic at AECL - and opened a rift between AECL and its private-sector allies in Canada. AECL's top negotiator flew to China to explain why the cabinet would front only $1.5 billion on a $4-billion project. The Chinese negotiators used that news to demand further concessions on AECL's package price for two CANDUs.

Back home, AECL officials were left to tell executives of the private nuclear suppliers in Canada - which had already been pressed to cut their subcontract bids by 15 per cent - that the $1.5 billion would have to be stretched even thinner. As the designer and patent holder on the CANDU reactor, AECL would need the lion's share of that money to complete the core China work. The response was fury.
With the deal about to collapse, China's chief nuclear negotiator, Li Yulun, took up an invitation by the Natural Resources deputy minister to visit Canada in May. The deputy ministers of Finance and International Trade were alerted. AECL drafted ``talking points'' for a courtesy call by Anne McLellan on Li Yulun. The lead suggestion was: "Demonstrate the prime

minister's full support for this project. It is important that Dr. Li is reassured that the prime minister continues to follow and support the development of this project."

The result was that the Chinese and Canadian nuclear negotiators signed an agreement, months *after* the Chretien cabinet approved the $1.5 billion, which meant AECL had lost the majority of the work on its CANDU project in China. It was now relegated to providing only the reactor core, and finding subcontractors for the balance of plant (BOP) construction and equipment supply.

For the Canadian private-sector suppliers, even more bitter news would soon follow. At Chinese insistence, they now had to compete with rival contractors being lined up by Beijing.

The Quebec nuclear suppliers threatened a revolt, and that was enough to compel Paul Martin, Anne McLellan, Roy McLaren (then the International Trade Minister) and Andre Ouellet (then the Minister of Foreign Affairs and the prime minister's long-standing Quebec lieutenant) to meet and discuss the imminent insurrection. In a letter to Ms. McLellan, her deputy minister noted: "Canatom and its parent companies (have) concerns -- particularly SNC-Lavalin -- over losing a significant contract on the CANDU project in China to Bechtel, an American competitor."

Given the hardball tactics the Chinese were using to play off competitors (including governments), there was no hope the Canadian private suppliers, or the Chretien cabinet, could reverse the Chinese decision to bid for sub-contractors. There was only one alternative: now AECL would have to give a portion of its slated work on the Chinese CANDUs to the private Quebec companies. The pie was getting sliced ever thinner. And so was AECL's profit margin, if there ever was one.

Still, the Chinese weren't happy. During the early months of 1996, they told AECL another $300 million must be cut from the price. The Canadians were aghast. Despite the conversion of former International Trade Minister Roy McLaren into a ``special envoy'' on the China deal, and a proposal by AECL president Reid Morden for a four-reactor deal to lower unit costs, another showdown on the CANDU sale price was inevitable.

It occurred in China in May 1996. There, Natural Resources Minister Anne McLellan squared off against Jiang Xinxiong, president of the Chinese National Nuclear Company.

100

Briefing notes from the meeting confirm the session was extraordinary. After the opening pleasantries, Mr. Jiang noted that ``the only remaining difficulty is pricing.'' Ms. McLellan responded that, "As the representative of the prime minister, she had to say AECL's offer was fair, and that there was little flexibility left. She had reviewed the components of AECL's bid. There may be a view that AECL has more room, but even a Crown Corporation has to cover costs, meet its budgets, and expect a small profit."

Mr. Jiang wasn't buying that. The economics weren't there. "He did not understand why there was no more flexibility. They could look at design, hardware and risk costs. These are a major part of the contract. There was still a big gap, roughly 10 per cent, or $300 million."

Ms. McLellan's turn came again. "Minister McLellan said she understood. (He) wanted to get the best deal for the Chinese people, but she still felt AECL's price was fair and competitive. It would be hard to do better," reads the summary. ``It was impossible for AECL to cut $150 million from the price of two reactors. The minister gave her personal assurance that we will do all we can to reduce the financing fees and to make AECL's package more competitive."

Then Dr. Li entered the debate. He pointed out that the French would supply cheaper reactors to China. ``On equipment, the primary pumps and balance of plant, steam generators and turbo-generators are all higher than the world price. The price is just not competitive. Some of this equipment must be changed during the (CANDU) plant life. On the Internet, he recently got information from India about (reactor) pressure tubes needing replacement after only 10 years."

Dr. Li's technical precision and hard bargaining apparently caused McLellan to falter. She suggested further discussions over lunch, but conceded ``there is some flexibility, but not much left. She understood there could be further discussion on financing fees. Movement is possible."

The de-briefing summary concluded: "The discussion continued over lunch. Dr. Kugler (of AECL) and Dr. Li explored some of the details of the divergences. There was some talk at one point of getting the gap down to $150 million (U.S.), and then splitting it in two. This would still leave the Canadians to find over $100 million Canadian."

Six months later, it was a done deal. Leading a Team Canada trade mission, Prime Minister Chretien clowned for the cameras in Beijing, did a little jig, and joked with Chinese Premier Li Peng at the ceremonial final signing of the state-to-state nuclear reactor sale.

But there was not much to dance about. Eventually, AECL and its Canadian contractors got only part of the whole loaf they thought they had bought. Both AECL and the federal government refused to publicly disclose key features of the $1.5-billion China loan guarantee, including the interest rate, repayment schedule, default penalties, exchange rate risks, government costs to cover the loan, and projected profit margin to AECL.

While Ottawa was preoccupied with hard-ball contract tactics from Li Peng's negotiators on the CANDU deal, proliferation experts and intelligence agencies were much more worried about China *simultaneously* selling sensitive nuclear and missile technology to renegade nations like Pakistan, North Korea, Libya and Iran.

These covert exports, and China's own nuclear weapons program, were arranged by the same national entity which approved the CANDU deal. Supervised for decades by Li Peng, the China National Nuclear Company seamlessly approved all military and civilian nuclear matters, domestic and foreign. In 1997, the U.S. Central Intelligence Agency concluded that globally "China was the single most important supplier of equipment and technology for weapons of mass destruction", and that it was Pakistan's "primary source of nuclear-related equipment and technology."[125]

China supplied Pakistan highly-enriched uranium, heavy water, tritium, precision uranium enrichment components known as ring magnets, lithium compounds used in H-bombs, nuclear-capable M-11 ballistic missiles, and a heavy-water reactor designed to produce plutonium for Pakistan's bomb program.[126] In fact, Li Peng had made several trips to Pakistan in the 1990's to discuss nuclear and missile technology transfers, while A.Q. Khan was concurrently making multiple trips to China, North Korea and Iran to acquire and barter nuclear components. Some of the hardware Khan bought was shipped home on Pakistani air force planes. Li Peng also led a trade mission to Iran in July, 1991, during which an oil-for-nuclear

---

[125] "The Acquisition of Technology Related to Weapons of Mass Destruction and Advanced Conventional Munitions", 1997, pg 5.
[126] Undated but documented summary by Washington-based Nuclear Control Institute

hardware pact was sealed and A.Q. Khan was designated the China-Pakistan-Iran conduit.[127]

After the 1998 Pakistan bomb tests, Li Peng claimed China had provided no help, when in fact the CNNC he directed was a chief supplier. Later, after Khan's 2004 arrest, Pakistan's Pervez Musharraf insisted that Khan's 'rogue espionage' had been conducted without his consent or knowledge. Yet Musharraf had been Pakistan's army chief when the atomic components were made and assembled, and Khan's bomb laboratory had been funded by the Pakistan military.

The most damning exposure of the China-Pakistan-Libya nuclear network came in October, 2003 when a cargo ship named the *BBC China* was intercepted by U.S. and British naval forces leaving the Suez Canal bound for Libya. The "used machine equipment" in the ship manifest turned out to be sophisticated uranium enrichment technology.
Also intercepted were detailed documents, a CD voice recording of A.Q. Khan explicitly discussing nuclear espionage, and blueprints for an atomic bomb China tested in the 1960's. Complete with hand-written notes in Chinese script, the seized blueprints were wrapped in a bag which originated from A.Q. Khan's tailor in Islamabad.

The dramatic *BBC China* seizure was publicly reported by a senior U.S. security official, John Bolton, and made global headlines. In February, 2004, Khan himself publicly confessed to his crimes on a Pakistan television broadcast relayed world-wide. Subsequent investigations by intelligence agencies, trials involving accused suppliers, and safeguards experts would leave no doubt that his import-export espionage network extended from Pakistan into China, North Korea, Libya, and Iran.

Nevertheless, Anne McLellan, the Canadian deputy prime minister who had vigorously promoted the CANDU sale to Li Peng's Communist regime in 1996, arrived in Islamabad in September, 2005 to make a similar Team Canada trade mission pitch to Pakistan's General Musharraf.
The following year McLellan left politics and became a director of Saskatchewan-based Cameco Corporation - the world's largest uranium producer.[128] Among its prime targets for future uranium sales were China, India and Pakistan.

---

[127] "Countdown to Crisis", Kenneth Timmerman; pg. 105-108
[128] McLellan was defeated in her Alberta riding when the Paul Martin Liberal minority government was replaced by the Conservative minority government of Stephen Harper.

CANADA'S INVISIBLE 'ELEPHANTS'

The 'atomic Wal-Mart' network of A.Q. Khan finally riveted public attention on the global dispersal of nuclear hardware during the past three decades, and brought overdue international vigilance on this covert commerce.

But it has inadvertently shifted scrutiny away from the accumulating world inventory of fissile *fuels*, and the deep flaws in international safeguards treaties which provide a civilian pretext for military programs.

No country has exploited this attention deficit disorder more than Canada. With barely a word of international alarm, Saskatchewan has literally staked out and delivered thirty per cent of global uranium production. Rich new reserves promise to keep that market share for decades.

The uranium sites in northern Saskatchewan are known as 'elephants' in mining parlance, because they are the richest on the planet. They lie in the Athabasca Basin sandstone geological formation, which is adjacent to the remote, hard-rock region that hosted the Beaverlodge uranium boom in the 1950's.

The discovery and development of the new Saskatchewan 'elephants' came because of two factors: sophisticated new aerial survey and mineral mapping technology, and the Trudeau-era uranium cartel. The former allowed mining companies to cheaply sweep vast areas and probe deep into geological formations hidden from pick-and-hammer prospecting. The cartel created a frenzied global rush to find new uranium deposits.

Among the early entrants to Saskatchewan's new, lucrative 'elephant' region were leading members of the illegal uranium cartel: Canada's federally-owned Eldorado Nuclear (later privatized as Cameco Corporation)[129]; the government of France (through Cogema Corporation, now morphed into Areva), and the Elliot Lake corporate giant, Denison Mines.

The stunning spike in uranium prices during the cartel era left these companies flush with cash, which they used to scout out or purchase northern Saskatchewan ore bodies. Rival companies also did this in Australia and southern Africa, where huge uranium deposits could be

---

[129] It merged with the province-owned Saskatchewan Mining Development Corp. in 1988, which owned interests in several of the richest ore bodies.

104

mined with low-cost open pit methods. By contrast, the Athabasca lodes were more expensive to extract - but the ore grades were many times richer.

This soon allowed Saskatchewan to gain a dominant market share in world uranium production, and made Cameco, Areva and Denison the major players there. When uranium prices fell after the cartel was exposed, these three predators were in the best position to swallow vulnerable non-cartel competitors, buy promising properties at distressed prices, and supply electric utilities locked into long-term reactor fuel contracts.

Another collateral beneficiary of the cartel was the government of Saskatchewan, which quickly cashed in on the new boom by claiming royalties on the uranium ore produced, or insisting on joint-venture deals with mine developers. In 1974, with cartel-induced uranium prices soaring, the NDP government of Allan Blakeney created the province-owned Saskatchewan Mining and Development Corporation. With the government holding the hammer over uranium mine licences and approvals, the SMDC leveraged major equity stakes in the rich new deposits.

This began when the SMDC obtained a 20% stake in the French government-owned [130] Cluff Lake project, which produced 62 million pounds of uranium before it closed in 2002. The SMDC then obtained a 50% interest in the Key Lake mine, which was then the world's largest and richest proven uranium deposit. Its ore was ten times richer than Cluff Lake.

By the early 1980's, the SMDC was involved in more than 300 joint venture mining projects, and had large equity stakes in the 'elephant' ore bodies soon to come. This put money in the provincial treasury but also created a glaring conflict of interest. While the Saskatchewan government was taking its royalty cut, or acting as joint-venture partner of uranium mines, it was also the regulator of new mine approvals and enforcer of environmental standards.

The fox was not only in charge of the henhouse, it was a co-owner. Not surprisingly, ethical questions about exactly where Saskatchewan's exported uranium was going, and what would become of millions of kilograms of resulting spent reactor fuel, were distinctly unwelcome.

---

[130] The French state interest was maintained through the subsidiaries Amok, Cogema and then Areva.

So was the idea of repatriating to Saskatchewan the plutonium and radioactive fission products that would remain lethal for centuries to come. For premiers of rival political stripes there was one point of unanimity: 'product liability' was somebody else's problem.

The cartel-stoked staking race in northern Saskatchewan peaked with the discovery of the Cigar Lake deposit in 1983, and nearby ore bodies such as McArthur River, Midwest Lake and McLean Lake. They would dwarf even the Key Lake deposit.

In 1988, the province-owned SMDC and federally-owned Eldorado Nuclear merged, then morphed into the private company Cameco. This created a uranium powerhouse endowed with operating mines, major equity stakes in the richest two ore deposits on the planet, and refining capacity to convert the raw "yellowcake" into the uranium-hexafluoride gas stage required for civilian reactors in the U.S., Europe and Asia.

No other entity could match Cameco on volume, purity, price, and milling and refining capacity. By 2008, it owned 232 million pounds of uranium at the McArthur River site, and 113 million pounds at Cigar Lake. The ore grades at both are twenty times richer than the Key Lake deposit. A single giant Cameco mill produces 18.7 million pounds of yellowcake per year, which serves fifty utilities in fourteen countries.[131] Virtually all of it is exported after being refined at Cameco plants in Blind River and Port Hope, Ontario.

The second largest uranium player is Areva, which in 2009 owned a 30% stake in the McArthur River deposit, and a 37% stake in Cigar Lake. They rank as the world's two largest, richest uranium deposits. Areva also has a 70% stake in the nearby McLean Lake uranium project. Between 1997 and 2007, Areva exported about 92 million pounds of uranium from Saskatchewan.

Areva also has a 67 % interest in the Midwest Lake uranium deposit, with former cartel-member Denison Mines owning 25%. It has estimated

---

[131] Cameco website, Marketing section, March 2009.

reserves of 41 million pounds of uranium, which would be processed into yellowcake at the existing McLean Lake mill owned by Areva.[132]

These combined Saskatchewan mines and mills will be able to produce about 27 million pounds of uranium for export each year, for decades to come. The world demand for uranium is slightly more than 100 million pounds per year. At a price of $70 per pound, those exports will be worth $1.9 billion annually.

The competition among these uranium producers is already cut-throat, leaving little incentive for loyalties of any kind. While Cameco has its headquarters in Saskatoon, it operates as a trans-national juggernaut seeking an ever bigger portfolio of bigger, richer, cheap-to-operate foreign deposits which might cumulatively come back to haunt even allies like Premier Brad Wall.

Cameco owns rich reserves in Kazakhstan, Niger and Australia. Areva also owns large deposits in Niger and Namibia, from which it plans to export uranium to India for six decades in a deal tied to Areva reactor sales.[133] The pending $1.2 billion uranium purchase, designed to thwart an Australian embargo on selling uranium to non-NPT signatories like India, was sweetened with offers to India of equity in the African uranium mines. If it proceeds, the Areva deal will also cut out sales of Canadian uranium and CANDU reactors to India. Meanwhile, Areva also cut a $12 billion deal to supply Communist China with two reactors and uranium fuel - another sales victory over its Canadian competition.

Similar predatory tactics, and the advent of huge new uranium projects from Kiggavik in Nunavut to those in Namibia or Russian Siberia, will likely keep the world price of uranium low. This will not be fatal to the existing 'elephants' of northern Saskatchewan, but it will give the uranium producers there increasing leverage to ask for lower royalties and taxes, and less stringent non-proliferation standards. Canada's decision to resume nuclear trade with non-NPT signatory India after a 25-year embargo, and seek uranium sales at the expense of Australia, is one example.

[132] Denison Mines Corp. website, November 2008
[133] Bloomberg, June 5, 2009

For the private Saskatchewan uranium producers which expect to reap profits until the ore is gone, and for politicians eager to claim credit for jobs, royalties and taxes for a few decades, the epochal perils embedded in the physics of uranium appear irrelevant.

Nevertheless, they will persistently prevail. The U_{238} isotopes comprise 99.3% of the yellowcake, and have a radioactive half-life of 4.4 billion years. The U_{235} content is less than 1%, and has a half-life of 704 million years. They are essentially immortal. When locked in its natural state underground, uranium poses no health or security threat to humans or other species.

But as soon as it is brought to the surface and concentrated, multiple dangers come into play. In northern Saskatchewan, the mining and milling process produces a 1:5 ratio of yellowcake to radioactive waste rock. While the yellowcake can be safely held in a hand, the discarded wastes have radioactive and toxic properties which will make them perilous for thousands of centuries.[134]

It is the sheer volume, the sinister nature of these radioactive wastes, and their longevity which makes them among the most toxic and hazardous of all waste sites in North America. For every 27 million pounds of uranium exported from Saskatchewan annually, about 120 million pounds of these radioactive wastes (as well as toxic heavy metals and acid leachate) will annually be dumped in excavated lakes, surface depressions or mine pits.[135] The wastes continuously generate radioactive decay elements, such as thorium-230 and radium-226, which emit diverse forms of radiation. These have insidious ways of concentrating in the food chain, mimicking key animal and human chemicals like calcium and iodine, and collecting in bones, organs or tissues. Once lodged there after ingestion or inhalation, they continue to emit radioactive pulses which can eventually cause cancers.

The projected yellowcake output from the richest Saskatchewan mines for the next two decades is about 540 million pounds, which translates into 2.7 billion pounds (1.2 million metric tonnes) of radioactive and toxic wastes. Engineering assurances that they could be contained in perpetuity behind earthen dams and dykes were crushed in 1984, when the Key Lake tailings dam burst and 100 million litres of toxic and radioactive waste escaped. The impossible happened a year after the mine opened.

---

[134] Report of the Joint Federal-Provincial Panel on Uranium Mining Developments in Northern Saskatchewan, October, 1993.
[135] Based on the average 1:5 ratio of yellowcake to waste rock.

An expanse of rugged boreal topography, sliced only by a single 700-kilometer access road, helps preserve a geographical disconnect between these mine wastes and Saskatchewan's largest city, Saskatoon. It serves as the headquarters for the major uranium producers, but for the rest of Canada the uranium 'elephants' and their lethal legacy are all but invisible.

There is a wider geographical disconnect which separates Canada from sixty or more foreign uranium customers of Cameco and Areva.

When it leaves the Cameco refinery in Port Hope, the uranium is in the form of a concentrated UF6 gas suitable for enrichment. It then becomes the property of the foreign purchaser, and its potency as a fissile fuel is essentially ageless. It could be inserted in a civilian reactor in a few months, or kept in its sealed state for five decades, or converted into a metal and stored for a century.

The gamble is that *none* of the 540 million pounds (245 million kilograms) of uranium exported as UF6 gas from Canada during the next two decades will be diverted for military use, or be acquired by terrorist groups in the centuries to come. The math is ominous, since the U_{235} content in that cumulative export volume is enough fissile material to make 88,000 Hiroshima-scale uranium bombs.[136]

This means that if only one per cent of Saskatchewan uranium exports during the next two decades is diverted for military or terrorist use, this would provide enough U_{235} for 880 warheads.

So there is zero margin for any safeguards failure. Yet given the huge annual Saskatchewan export volumes, the large number of foreign purchasers, and the limitless time liability due to the 4.4 billion year half-life of uranium, the odds are deadly. They are not improved by the fact that no Canadian or international body conducts actual audits of these exports - they disappear into foreign enrichment plants which co-mingle military and civilian streams.

---

[136] The calculation is 245 million pounds times .0072 per cent (percentage of U235 in natural uranium) divided by 2.2 (conversion to kilograms) divided by 20 (kilograms per bomb).

The proliferation implications of this will be examined later, but for now let us assume the highly improbable: that no Canadian U_{235} (from the exported $UF6$ gas) will ever be stolen, bought or bartered for military or terrorist use.

But that would solve only half the problem.

In the best case scenario, the Canadian uranium will be used in a civilian reactor and be transmuted into 540 million pounds of spent reactor wastes comprising 211 lethal radioactive fission products, many of which will pose a public security risk for millenia. This will occur regardless of reactor model, owner, or country of operation.

One of these Canadian-origin wastes will be plutonium, which has a half-life of 24,000 years. Given the projected 245 million kilograms of Canadian uranium exports during the next two decades, the cumulative plutonium content in the resulting civilian spent reactor fuel volume will be 637,000 kilograms - enough to make nearly 80,000 Nagasaki-scale warheads. Again, there is zero tolerance for safeguards failures.

But these risks of U_{235} or Pu_{239} diversion do not cancel each other out. Instead, they *double* the danger by raising the cumulative Canadian-origin fissile inventory which must be perfectly protected forever. A one per cent proliferation failure rate would mean some 1,680 rogue atomic weapons in the hands of someone, sometime, somewhere.[137]

So the presumption of zero illicit theft or diversion contradicts the arithmetic odds. The sheer volume of Saskatchewan's planned uranium exports *physically* defies those peaceful nations and world leaders who are desperately seeking ways to constrict the global flow of fissile materials, curtail new entrants, and cut down the number of atomic weapons.

While they are searching for a proliferation exit strategy, Canada is underwriting an encore.

The nuclear lobby has argued since U.S. President Dwight Eisenhower made his landmark 1953 "Atoms for Peace" speech that technical obstacles

---

[137] This represents the cumulative and combined U235 and Pu239 content in projected Canadian uranium exports for the next two decades.

and strict international safeguards can effectively quarantine off civilian from military atoms.[138]

After eleven drafts, it had undoubted eloquence and altruistic appeal.[139] It was delivered at the United Nations with stirring conviction, three months after Russia matched the U.S. by detonating its first hydrogen bomb. And there was added *gravitas* because Eisenhower, the former army commander who had led Allied forces to defeat Hitler in Europe, took as his theme the famous 'swords into ploughshares' passage in the Bible.

"It is not enough to take this weapon out of the hands of the soldiers," Eisenhower told three thousand U.N. delegates. "It must be put into the hands of those who will know how to strip its military casing and adapt it to the arts of peace."

There is no reason to doubt Eisenhower's personal sincerity. He was deeply troubled by reports from his military advisors that America and Russia would soon have enough weapons to incinerate each other - and that there was no defense against them.

"Let no one think that the expenditure of vast sums for weapons and systems of defense can guarantee absolute safety for the cities and citizens of any nation," he lamented. "The awful arithmetic of the atomic bomb does not permit any such easy solutions."

As a counter-measure, Eisenhower proposed that all nations be given access to civilian nuclear technologies on condition that they promise to sign agreements not to use them for making weapons. This global commerce would be supervised by a future U.N. safeguards agency, he suggested, which would solely control a 'pool' of fissile fuels drawn from American and Russian production stockpiles.

The basic bargain was that many nations would forswear atomic weapons and gain civilian power technology, while the two nuclear superpowers ratcheted down their arsenal production to the point of mutual elimination.

Eisenhower's "Atoms for Peace" solution was simple, elegant, and inspiring. It garnered near universal praise, and soon underpinned an unrestricted surge in global atomic technology transfers, technical knowledge and commerce. One early example was Canada's gift of the

---

[138] December 8, 1953
[139] "The Nuclear Barons"; Pringle and Spigelman; pgs 122-125

CIRUS reactor to India, and a larger CANDU to Pakistan. By 1956, the U.N. had convened the fledgling International Atomic Energy Agency (IAEA) in Vienna.

But words did not match deeds. The American atomic arsenal grew from 400 weapons in late 1950, to 20,000 by 1960, while Russia's increased from 5 to 1,600 during the same period.[140] By 1980, they had reached parity at 25,000 weapons each,[141] and Britain, France, China, Israel and India had joined the superpower club.

This sabotaged the *quid pro quo* in the "Atoms for Peace" pledge, and undercut the ethical authority of an IAEA tasked with both promoting the wide dispersal of civilian nuclear technology and preventing military diversions. But there was one technically astute group which publicly warned *before* 1953 that there was another fatal flaw embedded in Eisenhower's hopeful 'swords to ploughshares' premise: the Manhattan Project scientists.

They knew first-hand, from fundamental physics and their war-time bomb production efforts, that when Eisenhower sought to strip the 'military casing' of atomic bomb production and forge it into to the 'peaceful arts' of civilian reactors, fuels and knowledge - there were no changes to make. Except for actual bomb design, the reactors, enrichment and re-processing plants, scientific and engineering secrets, and fissile fuels like U_{235} and Pu_{239} were and are essentially identical.

This was explicitly conveyed in the 1945 scientific summary of the Manhattan Project written by Henry Smyth and published by the U.S. government. It was an accepted fact for Brigadier-General Leslie Groves, who commanded the war-time bomb project, and leading physicists like J. Robert Oppenheimer.

This knowledge moved to the political and diplomatic spheres in 1946, when U.S. President Harry Truman authorized advisor Dean Acheson to convene a select group to determine post-Hiroshima atomic policy. At the time, Truman believed it would take a decade or more for Russia to unlock the Manhattan Project secrets.

J. Robert Oppenheimer was the chief architect of the draft report which followed. Explicitly recognizing that it would be technically and

---

[140] "Bomb Scare", Cirincione, pg 26
[141] ibid, pg 36

diplomatically impossible to inspect and police unrestricted global nuclear commerce, he recommended that a single international body control or operate all uranium mines and production plants which could make, refine or process fissile materials. Small facilities for research and medical use would not be confined to U.N. control.

Acheson welcomed it as a "brilliant and profound" plan, but it was effectively sabotaged when Truman's bellicose secretary of state, James Byrnes, appointed a 75-year old Wall Street speculator, Bernard Baruch, to amend the report before presenting it to the U.N.

Baruch was instinctively hostile. The millionaire-banker assumed America could and should keep its monopoly on atomic arms, and rejected outright the proposal to put uranium mines under international control. He angrily annotated a copy of the report, writing in the margin: "This is a capitalist country, how can this plan be handled within our free enterprise structure without nationalization - which would endanger our whole way of life?"[142]

With Groves' agreement, the report Oppenheimer had drafted was stripped of its essential safeguards features in favour of a far more commerce-friendly model. Oppenheimer was appalled, and refused to join Baruch's scientific delegation to the initial U.N. conference considering proliferation policy.

"That was the day I gave up hope," Oppenheimer would later lament.[143] It was a historic opportunity squandered. The vainglorious Baruch dramatically took the stage at the U.N. conference and presented his revised plan as a take-it-or-leave it ultimatum.

The Baruch Plan argued for maintaining America's nuclear monopoly until a safeguards regime was in place. Five days later, Russia countered by arguing for America to disarm first, then pursue safeguards in concert with other nations. A diplomatic lull followed, punctuated weeks later by the detonation of a U.S. test bomb on the Bikini atoll - which Russian scientists had been invited to observe.

The sub-text was clear. Neither nation was seriously interested in arresting atomic proliferation. Truman turned to ramping up America's production plants, and Stalin accelerated the clandestine bomb project already underway in Russia.

---

[142] "The Nuclear Barons" pg 53
[143] "Oppenheimer"; Goodchild; pg 172

113

The failure of the Baruch Plan prompted the U.S. Congress to immediately impose a rigid but futile legal embargo on transferring any atomic technology, fuels or secrets outside the country - even to former Allies like Canada and Britain.[144] The same premise initially forbade private uranium mine production anywhere in America. The security risk was then considered far too high to allow any marriage of uranium and commercial motives.

When Eisenhower's "Atoms for Peace" policy reversal came in 1953, it rested on the president's newly assumed article of faith, not fact. The central tenet of his proposal - to place all fissile fuels under sole U.N. control - was reminiscent of the Oppenheimer proposal. But it was opposed by private uranium interests in the U.S., and quietly abandoned during the growing Cold War.

Nevertheless, the flawed "Atoms for Peace" premise underpinned U.S. policy for the next six decades, the safeguards mandate of the IAEA, and the future Nuclear Non-Proliferation Treaty. In the name of lifting the world's poor from poverty and making deserts bloom, atomic commerce would be consecrated as benign.

Thousands of technical papers were de-classified. Foreign scientists like India's Homi Bhabha and Pakistan's Munir Khan were invited to spend sabbaticals at reactor sites and plutonium labs like those at Chalk River. Uranium could be sold like steel, wheat or farm equipment. Plutonium-producing reactors would be designated 'peaceful' by virtue of promises made, not capability. There were even official IAEA blessings to detonate 'peaceful nuclear explosives' for diverting rivers and excavating mines.

All this was based on the illusion that a technical Rubicon could prevent the military and peaceful atoms from co-mingling. Tragically, it took two decades to first expose that fallacy when India confirmed - with Canadian complicity - that the peaceful atom was the perfect ruse for making nuclear bombs.

But by then the atomic genie was long out of the bottle, and there were already more India's in the making.

---

[144] The McMahon Act.

One of them was North Korea.

When it exploded a test bomb in October, 2006 [145], and then defiantly detonated an efficient plutonium weapon in May, 2009, it added a dangerous new dimension to the atomic arms race. Besides being a pariah state run by a psychotic dictator, it proved that even a small, desperately poor, politically shunned nation could produce an atomic bomb.

North Korea's test blast was also a powerful signal that the shape of the atomic arms race was changing. Just when the decades-old vertical build-up among a few known rivals was being reduced, proliferation was spreading horizontally to a nuclear-armed crowd whose members could stay anonymous until the day they detonated.

Most of the blame for this was placed at the feet of dictator Kim Jong Il, who now terrifies Japan, the U.S., and even former allies like Russia and China with nuclear-armed long-range missiles.[146] He has apparently provoked a regional atomic weapons race to solidify his domestic rule and orchestrate the succession of his son to power.

But it would be fatal to conclude that this was a 'lone gunman' event, or the aberrant act of a rogue state, or a case of atomic arms accidentally falling into the wrong hands.

In fact, North Korea fits the composite profile of a new class of renegade nations which purposefully use their NPT status as the very means to acquire atomic bombs, and cloak their intentions until it is too late. It was an NPT member for 13 years, and the first to renounce its membership on the eve of exploding a test bomb.

That this could occur is a scathing indictment of the NPT itself, and the 'paper tiger' safeguards function of its related International Atomic Energy Agency. Not only didn't IAEA inspectors detect, deter, and prevent North Korea's deadly mission, by their own statutes and operating codes they

---

[145] The atmospheric fission signature indicated a plutonium bomb. The explosive force was less than 1 Kt, apparently due to a poor implosion mechanism.
[146] North Korea announced in January, 2009 that it had weaponized its warheads.

couldn't. Worse still, this oblivious impotence has fostered the clandestine bomb programs of other NPT members like Iran, Libya, Iraq and Syria.

Although this has been minimally reported, these failures of the NPT and IAEA are an acutely important issue for the world community, and Canada. The global commerce in nuclear technology is predicated on the NPT and IAEA promise that military diversion can be detected and prevented.

Canada's annual export of seven million kilograms of uranium, and potential reactor sales such as those proposed to NPT outlaws India and Pakistan in 2009, rely on the same assurances. But if they are worthless, then the international trade in civilian uranium and reactors is effectively lawless.

North Korea's atomic end game should have been obvious to IAEA safeguards officials from the start.

Since 1945 the country had been ruled by Stalinist dictator Kim Il Sung, who had provoked the bloody civil war in the Korean peninsula and commanded a repressive, xenophobic regime until his death in 1994. His son, Kim Jong Il, would maintain the family tradition.

In the 1960's, the country had played off its two Communist patrons by obtaining an unsafeguarded small research reactor from Moscow, and help with uranium prospecting from China. It was already producing gram quantities of plutonium when it agreed to join the IAEA in 1974.

At that time, the IAEA director of nuclear reactor technology transfers to developing nations was Munir Khan, who had earlier negotiated the CANDU reactor transfer to Pakistan for covert plutonium production purposes. By joining the IAEA, North Korea qualified for access to technical training on reactor operations, uranium mining, fuel fabrication, plutonium separation, and spent fuel handling.

But North Korea kept producing plutonium from its first Russian-supplied reactor for another three years before it allowed initial IAEA inspections, and also sent a high-level observer to China's Lop Nor site to witness a test blast. In 1979, it began building a second 5 Mw reactor at Yongbyon, capable of producing six kilograms of plutonium annually.[147]

It was completed in 1986, the same year U.S. satellites detected a small plutonium separation lab and evidence of the high-explosives testing required for a plutonium-implosion device. Also under construction was a 50 Mw domestically designed reactor capable of producing enough plutonium for several bombs annually, and a larger plutonium separation plant. All were sanctioned by the IAEA and permissible under the NPT, which North Korea reluctantly signed in 1985 to qualify for the proposed transfer of two large Russian power reactors. [148]

But once again North Korea kept IAEA inspections at bay. It reneged on its obligation to allow site visits during the first 18 months after safeguards provisions came into force. The IAEA granted a second 18-month extension, which North Korea failed to honour. Meanwhile, plutonium was being produced and separated.

Next, in 1990, Kim insisted that his country would renounce its NPT membership unless the U.S. removed all nuclear weapons from South Korea. That bought time to begin building another large reactor, and covertly buy sensitive technologies from foreign sources.

When IAEA inspectors finally arrived in 1992, they found that plutonium production had exceeded that reported. When they asked to visit 'undeclared' nuclear facilities, they were denied, then Kim threatened (once again) to renounce the NPT. It took another year for the IAEA to formally report the 'non-compliance' to the U.N. security council.

This prompted Kim to suspend formal withdrawal from the NPT, and allow IAEA inspectors access to some sites - but only at night and with flashlights.[149] In October, 1993, North Korea again publicly threatened withdrawal from the NPT, and barred IAEA inspectors from the plutonium production reactor and separation plant. The IAEA reported that it could not assure the facilities were for peaceful uses.

In March, 1994, limited visits were resumed during which IAEA inspectors concluded North Korea had built a plutonium separation lab capable of

---

[147] U.S. Congressional Research Report, Oct 2006, Sharon Squassoni
[148] Russia was an NPT signatory, and so could not sell reactors to non-NPT countries.
[149] Wisconsin Project; North Korea Nuclear Milestones summary chart

doubling production. Months later, all the spent fuel from the 5 Mw reactor was processed, providing enough plutonium for several bombs. The IAEA then suspended assistance, and North Korea withdrew from the IAEA.

This triggered a diplomatic crisis, during which former U.S. president Jimmy Carter flew to North Korea. He negotiated an agreement which obligated the U.S. and other countries to provide $4.6 billion in financing for safeguarded power reactors, and donate oil supplies, in exchange for a freeze on further plutonium production and conversion.

This allowed IAEA inspections in North Korea to resume, which confirmed the stipulated freeze was being honoured. However, the IAEA was unaware that Kim Jong Il was covertly purchasing uranium enrichment technology from A.Q. Khan, in exchange for providing sophisticated Nadong missile technology (which morphed into Pakistan's Ghauri missiles).

The Khan connection was eventually discovered by the CIA, which reported North Korea's secret uranium enrichment facilities to the George W. Bush administration, and the IAEA in 2002. Caught, Kim Jong Il's officials conceded the truth, then sought a reported purchase of plutonium separation chemicals from China and removed fresh spent fuel for processing.

North Korea also ordered the IAEA inspectors to leave the country, withdrew from the NPT, restarted all its nuclear facilities, and moved a large amount of spent fuel to a separation plant. In February, 2003, once again, the IAEA reported the 'non-compliance' to the U.N. Security Council. More plutonium was processed, high-explosives tests continued, and technicians improved missile development.

In October, 2003, North Korea announced it had converted all the ostensibly safeguarded plutonium for warheads. Three years later, it exploded its first test bomb. By early 2009, it had enough accumulated plutonium for several dozen warheads, and was preparing to test advanced three-stage missiles with a range extending to Hawaii and Alaska.

The bare facts of the North Korea case implicate the IAEA as - at best - a dangerously oblivious enabler. Its mandate did not prevent it from dealing with two despotic dictators, or providing highly sensitive assistance to officials who served a military government. The IAEA inspectors were the last to question motives, or the malevolent character of the regime. The IAEA accepted repeated inspection denials and delays, acceded to segregated site visits, proved infinitely malleable when bullied, and failed to detect an entire uranium enrichment facility smuggled in under its nose by the infamous A.Q. Khan.

The IAEA prevented nothing. But this was not one exceptional botch job by the sole international agency entrusted to police and stop atomic proliferation. It was business as usual.

Of all the nations which actively abetted North Korea's bomb effort, then came to regret it, China is pre-eminent. What began in the 1960's as an example of Communist solidarity against the U.S. presence in South Korea had turned into its worst nightmare: rival atomic warheads on missiles only minutes across the Yellow Sea from Beijing, Shanghai and Guangzhou.

It took until June, 2009 for China to belatedly agree to U.N. sanctions against its former nuclear customer. But North Korea was not China's only covert client for atomic hardware and missiles. Seeking sub-regional partners to expand its influence, security, and military/nuclear sales, it courted an astonishing range of regimes.

While professing anti-proliferation goals at the U.N., Chinese agents and departments directed by deputy-premier Li Peng courted Pakistan, apartheid South Africa, Algeria, Argentina, Iran, Iraq and Syria. Among the components supplied were enriched uranium, enrichment technology, plutonium production reactors and separation labs, heavy water and heavy water technology, tritium and lithium (suitable for hydrogen bombs), brigades of technical assistants, missiles, and even designs for atomic bombs.[150]

The most alarming of all these worrisome China clients were Libya and Iran, because of the extensive, *simultaneous* involvement of A.Q. Khan and the IAEA. With subtle mastery, Beijing did its dirtiest work for more than a decade in two nominally compliant NPT countries, and proved that even the notorious Khan could flaunt IAEA safeguards with impunity.

The China-Pakistan-Libya-Iran links developed immediately after India's 1974 test bomb, which used plutonium from the Canadian-supplied CIRUS

---

[150] Nuclear Control Institute, summary chart of China activities.

reactor. While that appalled many nations, and acutely embarrassed Ottawa, it acted as a proliferation incentive for Pakistan leader Ali Bhutto, Libyan dictator Mohamar Qaddafi, and a Communist China anxious to counter India's new nuclear status.

After Bhutto flew to Libya to meet with Qaddafi and extracted a promise of millions in Libyan oil money to produce an "Islamic" weapon, he then flew to Beijing to meet Mao Tse-Tung to enlist China (which was clashing with India about the border region of Kashmir) to supply nuclear hardware and fissile fuels. [151]

Bhutto had also conscripted Munir Khan from the IAEA to spearhead Pakistan's bomb program under a civilian guise, and they personally escorted Colonel Qaddafi on a tour of the new CANDU reactor near Karachi to cement their tri-lateral plot.[152] Libya would bankroll a bomb for Pakistan and itself, and China would get most of the business.

Meanwhile, Bhutto authorized A.Q. Khan to steal uranium enrichment blueprints and supplier lists from a plant he worked at in the Netherlands. After his theft was exposed in 1976, he became the director of the Pakistani U_{235} enrichment effort at Kahuta (built with Chinese help), and the black market trader linking Beijing, Islamabad and Tripoli.

By the late 1970's the IAEA should have been on high alert about all three countries. Pakistan and China had refused to sign the NPT, and China was known to be assisting North Korea. Pakistan, now run by the dictator Zia al-Haq, was seeking a huge French plutonium reprocessing plant, an enrichment plant, and heavy water production capacity far bigger than anything matching its small civilian reactor fleet.

Libya's vast oil reserves meant it had no need for nuclear reactors. Among Arab nations Qaddafi was a leading opponent of Israel's nuclear status, and actively sponsoring terrorist networks.[153] The same year Libya became an NPT member, he vowed in a 1975 Lebanese newspaper interview: "The day will come when people say that this country has three nuclear bombs and that country has ten. When that day comes, Libya will not be absent."[154]

---

[151] "The Islamic Bomb", chapter 5
[152] ibid, pg 63
[153] Eventually, Libya would pay $1.5 billion as reparations for sponsoring the 1988 Pan Am airline explosion over Lockerbie, Scotland.
[154] ibid, pg 55

Finally, the 1974 India test bomb and the A.Q. Khan blueprint thefts - for which the Pakistani's name was on Interpol and European court alerts - had compelled a group of nuclear supplier nations (including Canada) to convene and draw up their own "trigger list" of technologies, components, fuels and exotic metals forbidden for sale without IAEA safeguards.

On the face of it, this was a laudable attempt by many vendor nations (known as the London Club) to tighten up nuclear exports by forcing their domestic suppliers to document the destination, purchaser and purpose of sensitive nuclear material. But it came with a fatal side agreement - countries which refused to sign the NPT but accepted IAEA inspections would qualify for these exports.

This not only expanded the scope of global nuclear commerce, but sharply reduced the diplomatic consequences for nations pursuing covert bomb programs. Unlike NPT members, if they were caught they faced no potential sanctions from the U.N. Once again, the commercial imperatives of the vendor countries had trumped proliferation goals, leaving the IAEA even weaker.

This had predicable consequences. Because China was not initially a member of the London Club or the NPT, it faced no diplomatic consequences for helping rogue nations, and it could remain an anonymous nuclear supplier, or broker deals through A.Q. Khan. Especially if a recipient country like Libya or Iran did not declare all their facilities to the IAEA, and the IAEA didn't have the inclination or authority to challenge the obvious.

This is exactly what happened in Libya. There is no doubt now that Colonel Qaddafi began attempting to build atomic bombs back in the 1970's - in part because he publicly admitted this after the U.S. intercepted a highly incriminating, February, 2003 recorded conversation between his chief atomic aide and A.Q. Khan. And a cargo ship containing sophisticated uranium enrichment components. And the actual blueprints for a Chinese atomic bomb.

This occurred when Libya was an NPT member in good standing. None of the discoveries were made by the IAEA. In fact, it was only after the 2003 seizures and admissions that the full extent of Libya's nuclear and chemical weapon installations (including 23 tonnes of mustard gas and ballistic shells) were discerned and dismantled by U.S. and British teams. Qaddafi had reportedly paid $100 million for the seized nuclear equipment, missiles and blueprints.

Belatedly, the IAEA sent an inspection team to visit four sites in Libya. It concluded that Qaddafi had assembled only the initial facilities needed for an atomic bomb, negotiated a new protocol authorizing future surprise inspections, praised Libya for being co-operative, and allowed its NPT membership to stand. No bomb actually detonated meant no harm done.

During the same period, China and A.Q. Khan also played a sinister, hidden hand in the atomic bomb effort of Iran.

Ever since it signed the NPT in 1970 and began negotiations to build two large German-supplied power reactors at the Bushehr site, a civilian reactor program has been an expensive incongruity for the worlds second largest oil producer. It has never lacked ready access to limitless, low-cost oil and natural gas for its electric grid.

The Bushehr reactor project was suspended when Islamic fundamentalists overthrew the ruling Shah in 1979, then was virtually destroyed in March, 1984 (before commissioning) by aerial bombing from Saddam Hussein's jet fighters during the Iran-Iraq war. Three years earlier, Israeli jets had inflicted worse damage during a surprise strike on the Osirak plutonium-production reactor Saddam Hussein was completing near Baghdad.

Now tensions had escalated further. Iraq and Iran were military foes, but shared a deeper declared enemy in an Israel which had forged its own nuclear warheads from the covert Dimona reactor. Mounted on Jericho missiles, they were aimed only at Arab nations.

Despite these hair-trigger military tensions, the ruthless and rigid character of the Islamic regime in Teheran, and the potential for future reactor bombings, the IAEA welcomed proposals to restore the Bushehr project. It granted millions in aid for damage assessments, foreign contractor re-construction, expanding domestic labs, technical training, uranium mining, and domestic fuel cycle development.

Ominously, in 1984 China helped Iran complete a new nuclear research lab at Isfahan which - without violating its NPT status - was declared off-limits to IAEA inspections. In July, 1985, China signed a $1.5 billion deal with

Iran to supply the Persian Gulf nation with missiles, jet fighters, patrol boats and military technicians.

The following year, A.Q. Khan publicly toured the Bushehr site and advised the Iranian military to replicate Pakistan's two-track path to atomic bombs. The Bushehr reactors could be used as a peaceful 'decoy' until they produced enough plutonium for atomic weapons, while Khan himself would supply uranium enrichment technology from China, North Korea and his espionage network.[155] While the IAEA would be watching Bushehr, these would be built with Khan's bootleg blueprints and operated far from prying eyes.

Months later, the Iranian government flew Khan to Teheran to sign a multi-million dollar consulting contract to provide his special services. The stolen Dutch enrichment plant blueprints - for which Khan had by then been convicted *in absentia* - sealed the deal. Then, after Iran signed an official accord with dictator Zia-al-Haq, Pakistani nuclear specialists began flooding into Iran to join Chinese and North Koreans involved in nuclear and missile production.

In January, 1990, Chinese general Jiang Xua arrived in Teheran to sign a 10-year nuclear co-operation agreement. It included supplying Iran with uranium enrichment technology, highly-enriched uranium, and a heavy-water plutonium production reactor. In July, 1991, Li Peng himself made a 3-day tour of nuclear sites in Iran where Chinese nuclear and missile technicians were working, and concluded his highly publicized state visit by signing a trade deal worth up to $5 billion.

In October, 1991, Chinese president Yang Shangkun arrived for his own tour of the Iran nuclear sites, then met days later with Pakistan military leaders to formalize the three nation nuclear supply chain. Beijing would get oil and cash, and Pakistan and Iran would continue getting nuclear production equipment, enriched uranium and UF6, bomb blueprints, and technical help.

By this time, the IAEA headquarters in Vienna had received a detailed German prosecutor's dossier on the Khan espionage network, and intelligence agency reports from the CIA and Israel's Mossad about the escalating Chinese involvement in Iran and Pakistan.

---

[155] "Countdown to Crisis: The Coming Nuclear Showdown with Iran: Kenneth Timmerman; pgs 36-41

A dubious Hans Blix, then the IAEA director, sent a team to Iran in February, 1992 led by Canadian official Jon Jennekins. With advance notification, and an IAEA concession to tour only some of the potential sites, the team returned to Vienna and issued a formal report confirming there were no suspicious activities. It later proved that the gullible IAEA inspectors had been taken to a decoy site - while Khan's covert enrichment equipment was nearby.[156]

The IAEA clearance further emboldened the conspirators. The leader of Iran's Revolutionary Guard flew to Beijing for another round of weapons purchases, then to North Korea to seal a deal with Kim Sung Il on nuclear component supplies, and co-development of a missile system which could strike Israel from Iran.[157]

The positive IAEA report also had the effect of reducing surveillance on the export of sensitive "trigger list" equipment from countries like Germany, France, and the U.S. to Iran. During the next decade it imported all the illicit components needed to produce enriched uranium, using the Khan network and a parallel operation featuring false-front companies, cut-outs, and 'turnaround' countries to disguise shipments to Iran and foil intelligence agencies.

Iran also enlisted Russia to complete the Bushehr reactors (still subject to IAEA inspections), developed its own uranium mine and milling operations, began constructing a heavy-water plutonium production reactor exempt from IAEA scrutiny, and continued separating plutonium from a research reactor.

In early 2003 satellite photographs and reports from dissident groups within Iran precisely identified several of the secret nuclear operations. Now facing acute embarrassment, an IAEA team headed by director-general Mohammad El Baradei flew to Teheran for the start of a tense sequence of inspections.

The worst fears were confirmed. On the first visit, the IAEA was astounded to find a vast uranium enrichment complex, comprising some 650,000 square feet, built deep underground for secrecy and protection from missile strikes. The Iranian hosts assured the IAEA inspectors that it was not yet commissioned, but test samples proved that false.

---

[156] ibid, pgs 110-115
[157] ibid, pgs 121-124

124

More IAEA visits followed, producing more lies and evasions. One inspection found traces of the exotic nuclear element pulonium, used as a neutron-rich trigger in hydrogen bombs. Finally, in October Iranian nuclear officials admitted to a host of undeclared facilities, including a huge UF6 production plant built with Chinese help, and the plutonium production reactor. It had imported more than 500 tonnes of uranium, and large amounts of UF6 gas for enriching. Still, they insisted, all was allowed under the NPT and every facility was for strictly peaceful purposes.

Incredibly, the IAEA issued a report in November, 2003 detailing the concealed Iranian facilities and fuels, but concluded: "To date, there is no evidence that the previously undeclared nuclear material and activities were related to a nuclear weapons program."

As diplomatic pressure mounted and receded over the next two years, Iran suspended and restarted its enrichment plants. It brazenly removed IAEA seals on key equipment, then reluctantly allowed them to be re-installed. Throughout 2004 and 2005, IAEA inspections found evidence of uranium enriched to 70 per cent, yellowcake conversion, construction of the plutonium production reactor, and evidence that Iran had been separating plutonium far earlier than declared.

Finally, in September 2005 the IAEA concluded that Iran was in non-compliance with the NPT and referred the case to the U.N. Security Council - at which China resisted quick, punitive measures. By then, Iran was supplying thirteen per cent of China's oil, and trade between the two countries had increased from $1.2 billion in 1998 to $9.5 billion.

In November, 2005, the IAEA publicly disclosed that Iran possessed a technical report on how to compress highly enriched uranium into spherical bomb components. Yet it took until the next summer for the U.N. to adopt Resolution 1696, calling for "Iran to suspend all enrichment-related and reprocessing activities" or face possible sanctions. In January, 2007, the IAEA terminated its technical assistance programs with Iran. More threats of U.N. sanctions followed.

But nothing stopped the defiant regime in Teheran, in part because the sanctions were sabotaged by a new $100 billion trade deal with China. It included promised assistance to develop Iran's Yadavaran oil fields and supply China with liquefied natural gas for 25 years. That mutual alliance allowed firebrand Mahmoud Ahmadinejad to proclaim Iran's peaceful intentions while thousands of whirling centrifuges kept distilling bomb-grade U_{235}, and nuclear technicians kept separating Pu_{239}.

Urban police forces around the world are judged by two basic performance indicators: the number of criminals caught, and the crime (or crime prevention) rate. Similarly, international anti-narcotics efforts are rated on the number of tonnes of illicit drugs seized, and whether the flow of narcotics is surging or being stemmed.

If these performance standards are applied to the IAEA, it is a glaring failure. It not only failed to prevent NPT members like North Korea, Libya and Iran from obtaining dangerous nuclear technology and fuels - it assisted them, provided a visage of legitimacy for decades, and was the last to detect bomb programs despite ongoing inspections.

The breadth and decades-long timeline of this pattern of failure indicates that better results will not be obtained with a bigger IAEA budget, more staff, or better on-site monitoring cameras and spectrometers spying for illicit atoms. It is not a question of technical competence, or corruption. Of implanting teeth in a paper tiger.

It *is* a question of physics, and of a fundamental conflict of interest embedded in the IAEA mandate, operating codes, and corporate culture which make it fatally blind to the obvious.

As the Manhattan Project scientists first discerned, and seven decades of nuclear arms production and nuclear commerce have confirmed, military and civilian atoms are elementally identical.

Canada's own history makes this point decisively. Our uranium mines supplied warhead material for American and British bombs for two decades, and the same mines later supplied uranium for civilian reactors. Our research reactors fostered benign experiments, but also plutonium for U.S. weapons and India's 1974 test bomb. Our CANDU reactors make electricity and plutonium simultaneously. The UF6 gas made at Port Hope was once enriched to bomb-grade purity at Oak Ridge; now it is being enriched to low levels for civilian reactors.

Nothing in this varied history has changed except intent. The Jeckyll-and-Hyde metaphor holds. His personality could change from altruistic to murderous, but both came from the same person.

126

This is precisely why the IAEA has been destined to fail from its inception. It was founded in 1958 on a hopeful but dangerous illusion that defied basic science, warnings from Nobel laureates, and technically impeccable documents like the Smyth Report. Using physics to underpin their proofs, they argued that military and civilian atoms were identical and interchangeable.

The primary IAEA premise, however, was that military and civilian atoms could be securely segregated, and that its inspectors would effectively police intentions. Given this, the IAEA interpreted the world-wide dispersal of nuclear technology (except bomb design) as a boon to humankind. It became the global champion of this cause, welcoming the idea that it must be shared among all nations, and written into the NPT as an inalienable right of 183 signatories.

This underpinned an IAEA culture of technological evangelism, which grew in mass, velocity and fervour during six decades as more and more staff were hired to promote the spread of nuclear technology as the chief means of preventing atomic weapons proliferation.

Eventually, this faith turned into blind conviction as the IAEA helped distribute nuclear fuels, technologies and sensitive knowledge to all corners of the globe. No dictator was too dangerous, or deranged, to receive uranium, plutonium, reactors, enrichment plants, or re-processing technology. No failed state or pariah regime was off limits.

Consider the chilling partial list of recipients of IAEA-sanctioned nuclear technology transfers. Iraq's Saddam Hussein. North Korea's Kim dynasty. Libya's Qaddafi. Iran's Ayatollah's. Argentina's junta leader Jorge Videla. South Korea's Chung Park Hee. In every case, we now know that these regimes had covert bomb programs. But the IAEA was the last to detect them.

Worse, despite the terrifying proliferation examples of North Korea and Iran, the IAEA has recently endorsed proposals to dilute already weak safeguards measures, further undercut the integrity of the NPT, and *reward* the very countries which used the "Atoms for Peace" ruse to camouflage bomb programs.

In this, Canada is deeply implicated. Reversing three decades of curtailed nuclear trade with India and Pakistan, it joined the U.S. and European nations in finessing terms to resume the opportunity to supply huge uranium and reactor orders. In a kind of diplomatic *pas-des-deux*, India and

Pakistan - now nuclear weapons nations - agreed to allow IAEA safeguards on future reactors and fuels while refusing safeguards on existing facilities of their own choosing.

This would allow the two non-NPT countries to continue building bombs, but preserve a non-proliferation visage by virtue of segregated inspections. The proposal was condemned by the U.S. Congress and most proliferation experts as a commercially expedient scheme which would subvert the NPT and incite other nations to build bombs with impunity.

But those countries with uranium and reactors to sell, and the IAEA, welcomed the plan. Even before the required bi-lateral agreements were signed, in early 2009 federal trade minister Stockwell Day[158] and Saskatchewan trade minister Lyle Stewart [159] were in India trying to land new contracts for large power reactors and millions of pounds of uranium.

Without safeguards agreements yet in place, Atomic Energy of Canada Ltd. enlisted an Indian contractor, Larsen & Toubro, to build a 1,000 Mw reactor which was still on AECL's drawing boards.[160] Saskatchewan's Lyle Stewart predicted that the 'elephants' in his province could soon produce up to 20 million kilograms of uranium each year, and invited Indian investors to cash in.[161]

If anyone asked, there would be no proliferation risk. These Team Canada exports would all be for peaceful purposes. The IAEA would be there to ensure that.

---

[158] Conservative MP and trade minister Stockwell Day led the trade mission to India in January, 2009.

[159] Stewart met with Indian atomic energy commission officials on Feb 18, 2009 in Mumbai.

[160] World Nuclear News, Jan 22, 2009.

[161] Saskatchewan for Stronger Economic Ties with India", Samay (India) news service, Feb 18, 2009

PLUTONIUM: THE IMMORTAL OUTLAW

On the face of it, the global nuclear power industry, and its supporting cast of governments like those of Canada, France, China and India, have a strong case that it offers an optimal - even inevitable - solution to the accelerating threat of climactic chaos. There is little doubt that even a doubling of world reactor output would produce essentially zero net greenhouse gas emissions.

Uranium contains no carbon, and that is being played as an invincible trump card. But the fervently faithful advocates of a nuclear renaissance virtually never mention the outlaw atomic element which can decisively smash that claim: plutonium. It is *their* inconvenient truth.

As a matter of physics, plutonium is created in every nuclear reactor of every make, model, size, purpose, or country of origin or operation - just as combusting coal in any power plant produces carbon emissions. It takes a mere 8 kilograms to make a Nagasaki-scale bomb, which fissioned a mass of plutonium comparable to the lead in a single shotgun shell.

So a doubling of global nuclear power will double the current world inventory of plutonium which has already accumulated in five decades of civilian reactor wastes, and in Cold War weapons stockpiles.

That plutonium inventory is now about 2,000 tonnes, or enough to make more than 225,000 workable weapons.[162] Most of it is in the spent fuel of civilian reactors, and each year the world's 440 reactors produce another 70 tonnes. Canada is a leading supplier of uranium for these reactors, and these exports effectively "embed" about 19 tonnes of new plutonium created annually. This is enough to make 2,300 bombs each year.

The arithmetic is awful, and obvious. Silently, invisibly, the world is becoming awash in a substance as sinister as the human mind can imagine, yet terrifyingly tempting to rogue states like North Korea and Iran. Or suicide bombers willing to deliver mega-deaths packaged inside a backpack, briefcase, or single-engine Cessna.

Each year, the odds grow worse that some of this accumulating, effectively immortal plutonium will be diverted by pariah states, or sold covertly for cash, or stolen for a bomb or nuclear blackmail. In 2009, the International

---

[162] ISIS "Tracking Plutonium Inventories"; Albright and Kramer; 2005

Atomic Energy Agency disclosed that its data base includes 1,646 reports of trafficking, theft or loss of nuclear materials since 1995, including 18 involving plutonium or highly enriched uranium.[163]

North Korea has proven that enough plutonium for a few warheads can be patiently extracted from a research reactor eight times smaller than that at Chalk River, then inserted into long-range missiles capable of striking Tokyo, Beijing or Hawaii. Recent reports document how it has passed this missile technology on to Iran.[164]

Despite this proliferation threat, Canada is playing the role of oblivious enabler. And, despite plutonium's deserved reputation as the most dirty and dangerous substance known, Canadian governments want to brazenly claim carbon offset credits while surreptitiously fostering more of it.

Plutonium is essentially a human invention. While remnant traces from past inter-stellar explosions likely exist in the vast universe, it took a brilliant combination of mathematics, physics, chemistry and engineering to produce the first micro-gram quantities here on Earth.

That happened in Berkeley, California in 1941. Spurred on by the pre-war surge in atomic research which had gleaned the secrets of fission, physicists had deduced that by bombarding uranium with neutrons a new, even heavier and more unstable element might be created as the U_{238} absorbed an extra neutron. This would make it element 239, which could likely be fissioned and release prodigious amounts of energy.

As Enrico Fermi's team raced to produce this new element with the world's first crude graphite reactor in an underground squash court in Chicago, a rival team in California bent to the task using a machine called a cyclotron, which used confined velocity to physically smash atoms together to overcome the binding force which kept their atomic integrity intact.[165]

---

[163] Associated Press, June 13, 2009.
[164] "A Technical Assessment of Iran's Ballistic Missile System"; Theodore Postol; May, 2009
[165] The California team was led by Glenn T. Seaborg. The cyclotron was designed by Ernest Lawrence.

The California team won the race by creating and distilling the first fissile plutonium, and later a host of other transuranic elements, with exotic names like americium and einsteinium. But the cyclotron was a formidably expensive, excruciatingly slow method of making plutonium. Months later, Fermi's first reactor proved far superior, and the micro-gram California sample was literally relegated to a desk drawer.

As the Manhattan Project gathered mass and velocity, vastly larger, graphite-moderated plutonium production reactors were constructed at the remote Hanford site in Washington state, and chemists turned to devising ways to extract the new fissile element from highly radioactive spent fuel. Eventually the locus would be the Savannah River plutonium production complex in South Carolina. Meanwhile, the Montreal atomic team worked on the heavy water reactor design, aided by the French chemist Bertrand Goldschmidt who developed what became the optimal plutonium separation process, called Purex.[166]

In every case this proved to be a dirty, dangerous quest. The plutonium could only be created in the heart of an intense atomic reaction, and then only recovered in trace amounts (along with unfissioned U_{235}) from within highly radioactive spent fuel assemblies. This required inventing heavily shielded labs and remote handling equipment to protect against lethal exposure from more than 200 different isotopes of varying radioactive intensity and toxicity.

Then, as now, plutonium re-processing required remote-control mechanical shears to cut open the highly radioactive metal assemblies which held the spent uranium fuel bundles. This unleashed fiercely intense gamma radiation, which immediately contaminated everything contacted and would have caused certain death within hours to anyone exposed.

Next, the spent fuel was dissolved in metal vessels filled with nitric acid and solvents to chemically dissolve, distil and purify the plutonium and unfissioned U_{235} isotopes from hundreds of other contaminated metallic isotopes. Because all this spent fuel was highly radioactive, it generated intense heat and was spontaneously explosive. So the acid bath had to be constantly cooled with a system of pumps, valves and extensive piping.

All this plutonium re-processing equipment - from the cutting shears to the distillation vessels to the cooling system pumps and piping - would become

---

[166] This chemical solvent process allowed the separation of both plutonium and uranium-235 isotopes from radioactive spent fuel.

dangerously radioactive after only minutes of exposure and would eventually have to be buried as high-level waste.

But the worst problem was and is the acid baths. To extract less than three kilograms of plutonium, one tonne of spent uranium metal has to be dissolved in constantly circulating acids, and this creates far larger volumes of highly contaminated, corrosive liquid wastes which remain not only permanently radioactive, but toxic, thermally hot and spontaneously explosive.

So scientists have known since the late 1940's that the price to pay for re-processing even grams of plutonium is a huge inventory of dangerous depleted reactor fuel, and a far greater mass of permanently radioactive equipment and solid and liquid wastes. Since the Purex method is essentially unchanged and remains the dominant method of plutonium extraction for both civilian and military uses today, this proportional environmental and public safety liability comes with every re-processing plant.

Then there is the plutonium itself. In addition to its overt weapons' proliferation risk, it is among the most toxic and carcinogenic substances known. As an emitter of intense alpha radiation, it can cause cancer at nano-scopic exposure levels, especially when inhaled as a dust or aerosol. As a matter of medicine or industrial hygiene, any exposure exceeds the bounds of safety.

Ironically, a hardened metal pellet of plutonium, or even a plum-sized sphere of the kind which destroyed Nagasaki can be safely held in a gloved hand momentarily, or shielded inside a leather briefcase. But these quixotic properties of plutonium also mean a kilogram can be covertly carried to the centre of a city, pulverized atop any tall building with ordinary explosives, and create massive airborne health damage and havoc without warning, and with little risk of detection.

In keeping with the aphorism that one man's garbage can be another's gold, for decades leading atomic scientists have been enthralled with the theoretical 'holy grail' of nuclear power physics: a reactor complex which breeds more plutonium than it consumes.

The central tenet is that plutonium is not a waste embedded in spent reactor fuel, but an asset to be recycled and burned to make unlimited energy. From this premise emerges the dream of a global commercial

132

'plutonium economy' which powers the planet, diverts plutonium from military use, and serves as the eleventh-hour means to avert catastrophic climate change.

This has an elegant appeal, and the physics involved have their own seductive 'technical sweetness'. Scientists have known since the Manhattan Project that fissile Pu_{239} can be both created in a nuclear reactor from U_{238}, and that it can also be used to bombard U_{238} to create more plutonium, or be used to transmute another non-fissile element, thorium-$_{230}$, into fissile U_{233}.[167]

Most civilian reactors like the CANDU or those used in the U.S. burn uranium in a 'once through' process, and the utility operators don't extract the plutonium in their spent fuel. That is why some 2,000 tonnes of plutonium have accumulated world-wide, which awaits a permanent disposal method yet to be invented.

But many nuclear advocates contend that this is glaringly inefficient, and a huge opportunity missed. The current 2,000 tonne plutonium stockpile could be used to fuel proposed 'mixed oxide' reactors, they argue, and the additional 70 tonnes produced by existing reactors each year could sustain them. Or, such plutonium could be used to "breed" virtually limitless global supplies of thorium $_{230}$ into fissile U_{233}, which could also power future reactors. Best of all, they contend, no carbon emissions would result. And this prospect has persuaded even notable environmentalists like James Lovelock to endorse nuclear power as a potential way to stave off climactic chaos.

There is little doubt this is technically possible. Since the early 1950's, U.S. and Russian military production reactors have used plutonium extracted from spent fuel to convert a surrounding 'blanket' of depleted U_{238} into more plutonium. This can also be done by inserting non-fissile U_{238} or thorium $_{230}$ target rods into civilian reactors, which are then transmuted into fissile materials. Prototype 'breeder' reactors already exist in France and Japan. Some are on the drawing boards in India.

But there are three flaws with this grand design: it will vastly increase the global stocks and flows of nuclear weapons-grade materials (U_{235}, U_{233}, Pu_{239}); it will inevitably magnify the volume of lethal wastes related to

---

[167] When bombarded with neutrons, thorium-230 can transmute into fissile U233 through rapid intermediary stages.

plutonium re-processing; and it will vastly increase the world's inventory of long-lived, highly radioactive (non-plutonium) spent fuel wastes.

Despite claims that nuclear energy can be a climate-friendly form of re-cycling, these fatal liabilities are embedded in any plan to create a commercial 'plutonium economy'. All fissile materials can be used in a civilian breeder reactor, or atomic weapons. All re-processing of spent reactor fuel involves separating and handling lethal materials, and generates immense volumes of toxic, corrosive, radioactive liquid wastes. And every reactor bequeaths long-lived wastes to future generations.

There is no lack of evidence to verify this. By 1996, the U.S. government faced spending more than $225 billion to clean up former nuclear weapons sites, including plutonium production plants at Hanford and the Savannah River complex in South Carolina.[168] The latter task, estimated to cost $100 billion, remains far from complete. Among the nightmare items are contaminated reactor cores, plutonium re-processing 'canyons' and separation plants, industrial equipment such as pumps and pipes, buried wastes now leaching into groundwater, and 100 million gallons of hellishly radioactive sludges, solvents and acid baths stored in corroding tanks and drums.[169]

A similar legacy exists at the U.K. military/civilian plutonium production complex at Windscale and related sites, where the clean-up cost is projected at $92 billion,[170] and at the French military/civilian plutonium processing plants at Marcoule and Cap la Hague. All are based on the Purex plutonium solvent-separation process developed by chemist Bertrand Goldschmidt in war-time Montreal. France continues to support exporting this technology to sustain future nuclear power plants built by its state company, Areva, in countries like India.

But the worst evidence lies in Russia, at a former plutonium production complex which Josef Stalin and his successors kept hidden from the world - and all but a few Soviet citizens - for decades. Built by 70,000 slave labourers and adjacent to former a "closed city" named after Stalin's

---

[168] "Atomic Audit"; Stephen Schwartz. His estimate reached as high as $410 billion.
[169] "Stewing Over Nuclear Leftovers"; research report, 2009; Max. S. Power. The U.S. nuclear weapons legacy includes 160,000 cubic meters of solid radioactive and hazardous wastes, 2,300 tonnes of spent fuel, and 38 tonnes of separated plutonium surplus to weapons requirements.
[170] Frank von Hippel; Scientific American, April, 2008

infamous secret police chief, Lavrentii Beria, it is known simply by a post-office box number, Cheliabinsk-40.

The complex included a heavy-water reactor directly modelled on Canada's NRX,[171] some graphite reactors, a prototype "breeder" reactor, and re-processing plants built to extract and separate plutonium for military use and "breeder" reactors. The latter left a level of contamination was so extreme, and a clean-up scale so daunting, Moscow invited a U.S. team to inspect the site in 1989 as the prelude to an escalating appeal for money and technical support. A sobering summary was later published in the Bulletin of Atomic Scientists.[172]

The secret complex was the site of a massive explosion in 1957, which contaminated a vast tract of land in the southern Ural Mountains. Highly volatile and radioactive liquid wastes left from plutonium re-processing exploded inside a holding tank after cooling water evaporated. An estimated 80 metric tonnes of highly radioactive residues detonated, spewing a plume of radiation equal to one quarter that from the 1989 Chernobyl disaster. Some 217 villages, and all water supplies, were contaminated. Earlier, high level nuclear wastes had been simply dumped into the adjacent Techa River. Later, radioactivity was detected as far downstream as the Arctic Ocean. The adjacent lake was also used as a sewer from the plutonium complex, to the point where it became so contaminated it had to be entombed in cement, waste rock and rubble.[173]

While these plutonium re-processing plants were built for military purposes, and operated during an era where environmental and safety standards were minimal, North Korea, Pakistan, India and Iran currently use essentially the same process to extract plutonium from civilian or research reactors. And any future civilian 'plutonium economy' would require dozens of similar plants using the same process and chemical ingredients, producing similar volumes of lethal wastes.

Despite the inescapable equation that plutonium re-processing and "breeder" reactors will inevitably create far more radioactive wastes than 'once through' reactors like the CANDU, many atomic apostles and even G8 leaders like George W. Bush, Vladamir Putin, Tony Blair and Stephen

---

[171] Used to produce both plutonium and tritium for Soviet hydrogen bombs.
[172] "A First Look at the Soviet Bomb Complex"; Cochrane and Norris; Bulletin of Atomic Scientists; May, 1991
[173] ibid; page 28

Harper have blithely contended that nuclear power is an "emissions free" boon to humankind.

In the months leading up to the crucial December, 2009 global climate change conference in Copenhagen, Canadian Prime Minister Stephen Harper and Saskatchewan Premier Brad Wall were publicly promoting CANDU reactors and uranium exports as worthy of massive credits to offset potential penalties for future carbon emissions.

Wall claimed that annual Saskatchewan uranium production displaced a half billion tonnes of greenhouse emissions, and that the pending Copenhagen conference should reward such heroism with credits which could be used to offset provincial carbon emissions, or cash in under a future carbon trading market.[174]

True to form, Premier Wall did not mention that those annual uranium exports would produce enough plutonium for some 2,300 nuclear bombs, and leave behind some 7,300 tonnes of radioactive spent fuel which would remain lethal for centuries.

Instead, he pressed ahead with an ambitious plan to become a dominant global exporter of enriched uranium, arguing that building a new plant in Saskatchewan would convert its booming export business into a 'value-added' enterprise supplying many of the globe's future reactors with low-enriched uranium. With global uranium enrichment capacity sharply falling, Wall's plan would guarantee sustained export sales with an effective tied-selling technique combining uranium supply and enrichment services.

If those enriched uranium exports could be matched to CANDU reactor export sales underwritten by Ottawa, all the better. And if all could qualify for massive carbon credits under the pending Copenhagen climate change protocol, even better yet.

But there were two fatal flaws to Premier Wall's grand plan: it ran squarely against President Obama's tough new global nuclear non-proliferation strategy, and such exports would directly compete *against* investments in future global green energy projects by pirating the value of carbon credits renewable projects would otherwise legitimately attain.

The new Obama anti-proliferation strategy was scoped out in Prague in April, 2009, then solidified at the following G8 meetings in Italy in July and

---

[174] Saskatoon Star-Phoenix, Jan 8, 2009.

136

in concurrent domestic U.S. decisions. In essence, it replicates the model Manhattan Project physicist J. Robert Oppenheimer had crafted immediately after World War Two to prevent an impending arms race with Soviet Russia. The central tenet was to confine fissile material production, processing plants, and global shipments to U.N. or multilateral control.

Coming six belated decades after Oppenheimer's original physics-based model was dismissed by Truman and Stalin, and emasculated by subsequent U.N. agreements, Obama's proliferation policy involves the infinitely more difficult task of getting the nuclear horses back in the barn, not just closing the gate before they bolt. Nevertheless, undoubtedly spurred on by the prospects of newly nuclear-armed North Korea and the imminent weapons status of Iran, he has taken bold and decisive steps.

In a July, 2009 meeting, Obama and Russian President Medvedev signed a mutual pledge to cut their atomic warheads to as few as 1,200 each, to reduce related missile and bomber strength, and to extend a multi-lateral comprehensive ban on weapons testing. Both the U.S. and Russia also agreed to destroy 34 tonnes of weapons-grade plutonium in each of their military stockpiles.

This was a clear signal to potential proliferating states that the two superpowers were finally matching their own rhetoric with actual atomic arms reductions. At the same time, they outlined a planned international protocol to sharply restrict the global flows of fissile materials, and reduce plutonium processing and enrichment sites.

In late June, 2009 the Obama administration also quietly shelved a George W. Bush-era plan to finance and build a proposed fleet of reactors dedicated to running on stockpiled and future civil-reactor source plutonium. This effectively ended U.S. entry into a 'plutonium economy' infrastructure, including new plutonium re-processing plants and "breeder" reactors. Aside from avoiding the egregious expense of building up to 75 special reactors at a cost of $200 billion,[175] this told other nations that plutonium processing and recycling was a dangerous dead end.

At the same time, preliminary permits were approved to build a private uranium enrichment plant in North Carolina which for the first time would deploy lasers to separate U_{235} isotopes from U_{238}. The new, privately-owned plant is meant to replace the output of several ageing, energy-intensive enrichment plants formerly built by the U.S. military, and supply domestic

---

[175] Frank von Hippel, Scientific American, April, 2008

and foreign civilian reactors with low-enriched uranium under carefully approved and audited contracts.[176]

As non-proliferation measures, both decisions would reduce the number of sites producing plutonium and enriched uranium, impose stricter controls on global conduits and customers, and fit within a proposed global "fissban" treaty to curtail dangerous nuclear material flows.

Ironically, one member of the consortium planning to build the South Carolina laser enrichment plant is Saskatchewan-based Cameco, which paid $125 million for its equity stake. Its powerful partners include General Electric and Hitachi. Cameco plans to route its Canadian yellowcake and UF6 exports through the U.S. plant, then supply American and European clients under the wary, watchful eyes of Washington and the International Atomic Energy Agency.

Apparently Cameco got the message that building such a plant in Saskatchewan, and exporting enriched uranium to any willing customer, was too big a proliferation risk for President Obama to tolerate. But as the Copenhagen climate change talks loomed, Premier Brad Wall was still pitching an enrichment plant for his province, and counting on uranium sales to wrack up not just revenues, but decades worth of carbon credits.

He claimed that Saskatchewan, as "the Saudi Arabia of uranium", deserved formal credits for displacing 500 million tonnes of greenhouse gases annually. If that were accepted at Copenhagen, it would preclude an equivalent volume of credits going to renewable projects, stall related green power investments, and drive down the value of all carbon credits because the sheer volume of uranium-based units would flood the carbon offset market.

Since these stroke-of-a-pen uranium-based credits would be created at zero incremental cost to companies like Cameco or governments like Saskatchewan, Canada or France,[177] they could be hedged and sold at future market prices to garner windfall profits worth billions annually. All while expanding the ambit and risk of nuclear proliferation due to more embedded plutonium exports, and increasing the world's accumulating stockpiles of latently lethal spent reactor fuel.

---

[176] Obama agreed to support a similar new enrichment plant in Kasakhstan to consolidate supply to Russian and Asian customers.
[177] As a condition of production or export licences, governments could claim such credits instead of the producer.

138

THE SOLAR CONSTANT

"Human society is too diverse, national passion too strong, human aggressiveness to deep for the peaceful and war-like atom to stay divorced for long. We cannot embrace one while abhorring the other. We must learn, if we want to live at all, to live without both."

Jacques-Yves Cousteau

Ten years into the 21st Century, humankind and the lovely, delicate planet we share confront two catastrophic forces: atomic proliferation spreading horizontally among nations because of unpoliceable nuclear fuels and technologies; and a climate crisis fostered by unchecked greenhouse gas emissions.

Canada is doubly implicated in this because Saskatchewan's uranium 'elephants' are putting millions of kilograms of fissile material on the open market each year, and Alberta's infamous tar sands are spewing millions of tonnes of greenhouse gases into the Earth's open skies.

As of 2008, after a half century of heavily-subsidized development, the world's 440 power reactors collectively met a mere five per cent of global energy demand - the same contribution as *wood* - or about sixteen per cent of electricity production.[178] Annual nuclear output was 2.6 billion kilowatt-hours.

The matching world annual uranium consumption was 65 million kilograms, [179] and the matching plutonium created annually in the radioactive spent fuel from these reactors was 70 tonnes [180] - or potentially enough for 7,000 bombs per year. These statistics are from the very nuclear industry which has recently re-branded itself as the "emissions free" white knight which can smite the scourge of greenhouse gases. That claim, and those numbers, compel some simple arithmetic.

Doubling nuclear power to ten per cent of world energy demand would require some 900 reactors to be in operation, which would consume 120

---

[178] "The Next Wave of Nuclear Proliferation"; Nader Elhefnawy; 2008
[179] World Nuclear Organization, Uranium fact sheet, March, 2009. Some of the uranium consumed came from stockpiled sources. Canada accounted for about 30 per cent of new production.
[180] World Nuclear Orgaization, Plutonium fact sheet, March, 2009

million kilograms of uranium annually and create enough plutonium for 14,000 warheads *each year*. By comparison, the existing world total of nuclear warheads is 27,000.

If it is assumed that 900 future civilian reactors would have an average life-span of three decades, enough cumulative plutonium for 420,000 warheads would be the collateral cost of meeting ten per cent of global energy demand for a few decades.

These numbers belie the nuclear industry's claim that its vaunted renaissance will slay the dragon of greenhouse gases. It is technically and financially *impossible* for nuclear plants to replace the 86 per cent of global energy now supplied by fossil fuels. Replacing only five per cent would create an extra proliferation liability lasting hundreds of centuries. This is no less harrowing because it is buried in the fine print.

An energy strategy which merely substitutes plutonium tommorrow for carbon pollutants today amounts to trading fatal poisons. So, despite the daunting task, human survival depends on devising an exit strategy from both.

Luckily, there is an astonishing, elegant way to do this - with thermonuclear explosions. Actually, millions of them constantly occurring 93 million miles away from Earth. There, stupendous gravitational forces and immense heat crush hydrogen into helium atoms, releasing neutrons which ignite more implosions which fuse heavier and heavier elements in a swirling, self-contained fireball. As the electromagnetic forces which separate atoms are unceasingly smashed, heat, light, and radiant energy stream outward.

This solar reactor already provides our planet far more daily energy than all the uranium and fossil fuels humans burn. As calculated by physicists, the 'solar constant' of radiation hitting the Earth's surface at any given time converts into the electricity equivalent of an astounding 5×10^{7} Megawatts per *second*, [181] or an average 1,366 watts per square meter of the planet's surface.

No scientist seriously disputes this number. Despite the imposing, virtually impossible-to-imagine scale of this sum, for physicists it is a rather elementary equation.

---

[181] Lovelock, James: Gaia: A New Look at Life on Earth; pg 140

One way to put this number in a human dimension is to say that this solar radiation has enough latent energy to constantly power the world climatic cycles, produce oceans full of fish and plants, generate every tree of every forest, grow every grain and blade of grass, and provide food and heat for almost two million animal species and 6.6 billion people. It also drives all forms of solar power technology, wind and hydro-electric turbines, and underpins energy obtained from biomass, or biofuels. For our sun, that is literally all in a day's work.

Put another way, the solar energy hitting the Earth's surface exceeds the explosive power of 100 million Hiroshima-scale blasts. Every second. Like all matter, both the sun and thermonuclear bombs obey the laws of physics revealed in Einstein's famous $E=mc^2$ equation. The only difference is that the sun's chain reactions never stop, and explode at a discreet distance.

Although it is invisible, the resulting solar radiation reaching the Earth is as material and constant as uranium. Its energy value can be measured as precisely as that of neutron bursts when atoms are split. And so it has immense survival value, because if humanity can craft ways to harness even a few per cent of this inexhaustible energy bounty, then fossil fuels, uranium, and even nuclear weapons - which are fostered by geo-political disparities - all become irrelevant. Nations will fight over oil, but not sunshine.

For the instinctively sceptical, or the technology obsessed, it might help if the sun were re-branded as a thermonuclear reactor, a solar engine, an offshore hydrogen deposit, or a photon factory which couriers its just-in-time product in the same way signals are beamed from satellite to receiver. This can instantly shift the conceptual terrain. Benign sunshine becomes wealth. The hippie's high hope becomes an engineer's challenge.

But regardless, the physics of solar thermonuclear energy await being applied just as seven decades ago Manhattan Project scientists unlocked what Robert Oppenheimer called the "technically sweet" secrets of controlled fission. The quest is even more alluring because if it is successful, humanity might eliminate the triple threats of climate change, radioactive risks, and atomic warfare.

Yet many major players in the global energy field argue that solar power is preposterously unqualified to power any modern industrial society.

On the face of it, their case is strong. The amount of sunlight which can be converted into electric power on a household photo-electric panel is typically less than one hundred watts. By contrast, a nuclear reactor can produce one million watts. The daily world electricity power demand is billions of watts, and growing. More fossil energy is used to fuel cars, trucks, ships and airplanes. More still is burned to heat homes and power industries.

Using this prevalent point of reference, solar energy can be quickly consigned to green boutique status while the future heavy lifting is left to nuclear, oil, natural gas and coal - with escalating proliferation and climate chaos as inevitable collateral damage. But there are five problems with this crude model of analysis, which has a pre-ordained conclusion embedded in the premise.

First, it will deliver climatic or atomic calamity, or both. Second, contrasting one solar panel with one nuclear plant is like comparing one apple and one thousand oranges. It would be more accurate to compare one solar panel and a 5-milligram uranium reaction, or a Saharan or Saskatchewan solar park covering 10 square miles to a nuclear plant. Third, it does not compare the performance efficiency. Fourth, it does not compare the applicability to energy needs. And finally, it does not compare the complete costs per unit of energy actually delivered.

In short, the prevalent solar panel *versus* nuclear plant comparison does not test for actual *value* - it assumes only size matters and produces an inevitable conclusion: bigger is better. But counter-intuitive scrutiny compares each for size, performance, cost, relevance, environmental integrity, and related risks of catastrophe.

How does this play out in the real world?

Canada's proposed exports of reactors and uranium are often justified on the grounds that developing countries desperately need the power, and are morally entitled to the best of modern science and engineering. In early 2009, exactly those arguments were made during missions to India by Canada's federal and Saskatchewan trade ministers.

But one third of humanity, including 400 million rural poor in India and 25 million in Brasil, are not even connected to electric grids, won't be for decades at best, and can't afford hook-up charges and the monthly bills of $70 or more required to pay for nuclear power. These 2.2 billion people typically earn $70 per month - which means their entire income would be spent on electricity alone. Yet most live in equatorial or sub-tropic regions

142

with free access to the solar wealth streaming onto their rooftops and fields each day.

One of the most pressing needs in India is to replace more than four million diesel-powered water pumps with solar systems in rural regions where there is no electric grid. The inefficient, expensive-to-operate, and dirty diesel pumps are used for crop irrigation, sanitation, and village water supply. Despite their life-time operating cost advantage, higher reliability, and pollution reduction benefits, only some 7,000 multi-panel solar pump systems have been installed to replace diesel pumps. The chief obstacle is the dearth of purchasing capital.

For rural populations in India, and the poorest one-third of humanity, a nuclear plant with no grid to connect them is as preposterous as selling a remote Amazon villager a Hummer when there are no roads, no gas, and nowhere better to go.

The huge scale and engineering costs needed to contain a nuclear reaction are completely mismatched to rural scales and needs. There is often no grid to carry the power, and those that do exist can typically transmit only a few thousand kilowatts. Replacing them with high-voltage lines and transformers would bankrupt most local utilities. And reactors tend to be highly unreliable - the performance of other reactors in India or Pakistan has been dismal due to endemic breakdowns, parts shortages, and lack of specialized training.

Meanwhile, household solar panel packages with a battery, water pump and lights can be currently leased in India or Brasil for about $10 per month. A second panel costing $5 per month can power a small fridge. They can also be assembled, installed and maintained by local labourers.

Like the now ubiquitous cell phones, these leased solar kits eliminate hard-wired dependence on utilities, or the often bribeable beneficence of officials deciding where grids might be built, or hook-ups approved. The battery storage helps calibrate delivery and demand, and can be adapted for tasks like grinding flour or garden irrigation. They produce no bomb-grade plutonium, lethal radioactive wastes or greenhouse gases.

It is no over-statement to say that these rooftop solar systems can bring millions of impoverished families from the 19th Century to the 21st Century in the few hours it takes to install them. Often, the cost can be financed through micro-credit sources like the Grameen Bank, or non-profit foundations like that of Fabio Rosa in Brasil. By contrast, CANDU plants typically take more than a dozen years to construct, and come with chronic cost overruns.

India also has spectacular potential for large-scale, grid-connected solar farms in its arid northern interior and equatorial regions, or wind farms along its immense coastline. The combination of high average daily solar gain (4,000 to 7,000 watts per square meter) and dense population is optimal. The theoretical potential exceeds total current national electricity demand, although it took until May, 2008 for the federal government in Delhi to adopt incentives to foster this potential.

But a picture of what is possible can be gleaned from its rival China, which is far ahead of India despite lower quality average solar gain. More than 30 million Chinese households already use low-cost rooftop solar systems which directly heat domestic hot water instead of making electricity. They typically cost $200, and displace electric or fossil-fired hot water heaters. The combined thermal power from these solar systems converts to the electric equivalent of nearly forty power plants.[182]

China is also the world powerhouse in producing and exporting solar photovoltaic panels, which can convert sunlight into electricity on individual rooftops, or be aggregated into commercial arrays or grid-connected power plants up to 500 megawatts. The annual production of modules (measured by electrical output) grew from 1.2 megawatts in 1994, to 1,600 megawatts by 2008.[183]

The global increase in solar PV installations is nothing short of breathtaking. Underpinned by improved efficiency, innovations in new materials, and lower costs due to mass production lines, the installed price per peak watt has dropped from $27 in 1982 to under $4. When it drops to $3 per peak watt, emissions-free solar PV 'farms' will be price competitive with large polluting coal plants.

The world-wide power output from combined new solar photovoltaic installations in 2008 totalled nearly 6,000 megawatts - a 110 per cent increase over 2007.[184] This generated $37 billion in global revenues. Although Europe accounts for 88 per cent of these installations, village-scale solar PV projects are being built in China, India, Malaysia, Nepal,

[182] Perlin, John: "From Space to Earth: The Story of Solar Electricity".
[183] Photon International, October, 2008
[184] Solarbuzz World Market Report, March, 2009

Ghana and Latin America where performance is not the obstacle - it is a lack of purchasing capital.

Based on merit, or the 'stress test' scores on price, performance and pollution reductions, solar hot water and solar PV are a leading solution for solving energy and poverty problems in developing nations. They can most quickly match the needs of the poorest.

By contrast, CANDU reactor sales to nations like India and Pakistan mask self-interest beneath a veneer of benevolence. They may be a winner for the seller, but they are a loser for the ultimate customers - not least because they rob poor economies of the scarce capital needed to adopt quicker, more agile, smarter and safer solutions.

The same 'stress test' for composite value is increasingly costing the nuclear reactor industry world-wide defeats in head-to-head competition with renewables and energy efficiency. Far from a surging renaissance, many nuclear players are in retreat while green power cost-performance curves and market share are on a steep ascent.

The thrilling evidence is everywhere. Globally, investments in the renewables sector were $155 billion in 2008, while revenues from solar, wind and biofuels climbed from $75.8 billion in 2007 to $115.9 billion.[185] Of that revenue total, solar accounted for $29.6 billion and wind power accounted for $51.4 billion (all $U.S.) According to Clean Edge investment analysts, annual global renewable revenues will almost triple to $325 billion by 2018.

This is not the profile of a boutique business. It's a clear and present danger to nuclear rivals.

In 2006, nuclear plants world-wide increased 1.4 billion watts in net capacity. This was less than additions by solar-electric panels, one-tenth of additional world wind farm power, and one thirtieth of the combined contribution of de-centralized or 'micro-power' production.[186]

[185] "Clean Energy Trends" report, by Clean Edge; March, 2009
[186] Amory Lovins, chief scientist, Rocky Mountain Institute, interview on National Public Radio, July, 2008. The decentralized energy total includes combined heat and power (cogeneration) but does not include large hydro.

This surge in renewable energy installations has accelerated since. In 2008, global renewable energy investments reached $120 billion, a four-fold increase since 2004. Grid-connected solar photovoltaic capacity grew by 70 per cent, installed wind power capacity grew by 29 per cent, solar hot water output grew by 15 per cent, and biofuel production rose by 34 per cent. Other contributions came from small hydro and geothermal.[187]

The United States accounted for one fifth ($24 billion) of the 2008 global renewable energy investment, and led the way in new wind, grid-connected solar installations, and geothermal projects. European countries followed, but China, India and Brazil showed the most meteoric rates of growth. China's installed wind capacity has doubled each year since 2004, it now leads the world in solar hot water installations, and has become the world's biggest producer of solar photovoltaic panels. India ranked third in new wind capacity installed. Brazil remained a top producer of biofuels. [188]

Ranked by combined new capacity added in 2008 from all renewable technologies, China ranked first. It was followed by the U.S., Germany, Spain, India and Japan. Developing countries accounted for 43 per cent of the new installations, which totalled 40,000 megawatts in 2008. Renewable energy capacity has now reached 280,000 megawatts world-wide.[189] That compares to a total existing nuclear capacity of about 14,000 megawatts in Canada.

The $120 billion invested in global renewables in 2008 compared to $63 billion invested in 2006. The leading technology sectors were wind ($51.8 billion), solar-photovoltaic ($33.5 billion), and biofuels ($16.9 billion). The U.S. ranked first in new investments, followed by Spain, China, Germany and Brazil.[190] Among developing countries, China has recently pledged $15 billion to support green power technologies, and Morocco $1 billion.

Despite the world-wide recession which hit in the fall of 2008, an authoritative report on green technology investment trends predicts strong growth in the near future. The leader will likely be solar-photovoltaic, for which prices are projected to decrease by 43 per cent in 2009 due to new

---

[187] Worldwatch REN 21 Renewables Global Status Report, 2009, Executive Summary
[188] ibid, pg 9
[189] ibid, pg 12
[190] ibid, pg 14

production capacity and lower per-watt costs due to cheaper materials and more efficient manufacturing techniques.[191]

According to physicist and energy analyst Amory Lovins, combined output from thousands of small micro-power projects now outstrips annual new nuclear capacity in China, and annual new coal plant output in the U.S.

This startling picture only emerged when astute analysts like Lovins, Clean Edge, and the World Association for De-Centralized Energy (WADE) began applying the venerable adage that one hundred pennies has the same value as one dollar. Instead of dismissing individual micro-power projects as inconsequential 'pennies', they drilled down into the disaggregated global energy, financing and construction data to discover where the 'dollars' were both hiding and flowing.

At the same time, investment rating agencies like Moody's Investor Services predicted sky-rocketing costs for new nuclear plants, while impartial agencies like the U.S. General Accounting Office and Congressional Budget Office projected an alarming fifty per cent default rate risk on prospective federal loans for nuclear projects.[192]

This explains why no firm reactor orders have been placed by U.S. private electric utilities since 1978, and the last plant to be commissioned, in 1996, was ordered in 1970.[193] The utility shareholders won't tolerate the risks. While overall operating performance has increased in recent years, other nuclear plant closings due to dismal performance means there has been no net additions in U.S. nuclear capacity since 1988.

The huge capital costs, 15-year licencing and construction timeline, uncertain debt and interest payments, and risk of escalating radioactive waste disposal costs (now projected at $100 billion for civilian and military nuclear wastes) have stalled U.S. utility applications to build more. When requested federal tax credits for nuclear plants worth $50 billion were cut out of the February, 2009 Obama administration stimulus package, just as bank credit tightened dramatically, the U.S. nuclear industry likely suffered the equivalent of a stroke caused by fatal finances.

---

[191] Growing Trends in Renewable Energy Investment 2009; New Energy Finance
[192] Nuclear Power: The Outlook for New U.S. Reactors, Congressional Research Service, March 2007
[193] ibid, pg 4

Perhaps nothing symbolized the rising fortunes of renewable energy better than the 2008 declaration by famed Texas oil tycoon T. Boone Pickens that he would invest $10 billion or more to develop wind farms in his home state and the blustery mid-west corn belt running all the way north to Saskatchewan. His reasons were blunt: to make money and reduce American dependence on foreign oil.

But Pickens was not the only unlikely green power convert. California governor Arnold Schwartzenegger has spear-headed renewable and energy efficiency initiatives designed to decisively cut carbon emissions without building any new nuclear plants. This is no small feat, since California has a population equal to that of Canada and is the world's eighth largest economy.

Yet this will continue an innovation trend already deeply embedded in the state regulatory culture, which has kept California per capita electricity use at 1975 levels. An integrated package of better planning, efficiency standards, building codes, regulations, customer incentives, and accurate pricing produced a conservation 'dividend' of 10,000 megawatts in demand reductions. This eliminated the need to build twenty power plants.[194]

This success was accelerated by the punishing power blackouts of 2001, and premised on the fiscal evidence that it is almost always cheaper, quicker and cleaner to invest in efficiency than build new power plants to supply wasted energy. So California planners calculated the relative costs of "buying" a portfolio of efficiency measures, and compared those to what ratepayers would eventually pay for a range of new renewable, gas, or nuclear power plants. They also calculated how fast each could be delivered.

It was no contest. The composite value of conservation out-competed even renewable energy investments. New nuclear capacity was the most expensive option - and could not deliver any power until a decade after licensing approval might be obtained. For a state facing imminent blackouts and a severe budget crunch, this was fatal.

Two years after more intensive efficiency programs began, summer peak use fell by up to 5,300 megawatts because the California private utilities *paid* their residential, commercial and industrial customers to reduce consumption. The incentive worked by promising customers a 20 per cent reduction in their bill for reducing demand by 20 per cent.

---

[194] California Energy Commission and Bachrach, Ardema, Leupp, "Energy Efficiency Leadership in California: Preventing the Next Crisis", NRDC, 2002.

148

The customer take-up rate was huge. It not only averted imminent blackouts, but saved Californians $660 million in punitive peak pricing, while reducing carbon dioxide pollution by 8 million tonnes and smog-forming nitrogen oxides by 2,700 tonnes. This was the equivalent of taking 1.5 million passenger vehicles off the road for one year.[195]

Since then, putting more money and muscle into energy efficiency has kept California in the lead. More recent reports indicate conservation can capture a further 3,500 megawatts in demand reductions, at a net saving of $8.6 billion. This could eliminate the need to build another seven 500 Mw power plants, and has pushed the future of nuclear power in the Golden State beyond the horizon.

The final nail will likely be delivered by an equally impressive surge in renewable energy projects in California. It pioneered some solar and wind power projects in the 1980's, but a loss of valuable tax credits stalled most development in the 1990's and left the state exposed to blackouts.

That was reversed, then project investments revived with the high-profile support of renewable energy's new champion, Governor Schwartzenegger. He accelerated aggressive policy measures, including firm targets for utilities to ensure new, diverse, in-state renewable projects comprised a minimum 20 per cent of generation by fixed dates. The utilities were left to choose which green power technologies and companies to contract with, and negotiate their own prices and terms.

This fostered a torrent of project proposals, intense competition, and renewable project innovation including the marriage of intermittent green power like wind and solar, with advanced storage technologies which could 'bottle' the power for on-peak delivery. The California utilities could seek and deploy any combination which was cheaper than the premium priced-power they would otherwise buy during peak demand.

This caused investment to flow into the green power projects, advanced storage technologies from fuel cells to flywheels, and also pioneering 'smart grid' technologies which could calibrate supply and demand in milliseconds to make more efficient use of the transmission grid. Like traffic lights, this allows more green projects to link up to a constrained network, and in some cases avoids the need to build expensive new transmission lines or transformers.

---

[195] Ibid NRDC

The 'green rush' in California has accelerated because of firm regulatory measures promoting increased grid-connected renewable projects for utilities, and a $3.3 billion program for residential and commercial solar PV installations. These new markets have ignited investment, entrepreneurship, and technology innovation similar to that in California's Silicon Valley a generation earlier.

Seeking economies of scale, solar 'prospectors' now scout out urban buildings such as shopping malls, big box stores, schools and giant distribution warehouses to lease rooftop space for large solar PV arrays. Those allow solar parks without taking up valuable land, and give the building owners added income for what was otherwise worthless space. At the same time, utilities and non-profit groups are conscripting thousands of California residences, commercial and public buildings for smaller solar PV or solar hot water installations.

This burgeoning market, which has spread eastward through Arizona and Texas to Florida, has recently vaulted the U.S. into the world's largest installer of solar-electric panels. Now it is attracting billions in investment capital for ultra high-tech factories to mass produce the solar PV panels, and has helped to ramp up global production of the components and materials.

The resulting lower unit costs, and the built-in ability of solar panels to be connected in sequence and scaled to any size, means the same solar panel production factory can supply four panels for a residential roof, or forty-thousand panels for a solar park.

In 2008, California's dominant private utility, Pacific Gas and Electric, announced a landmark contract to buy solar-electric power from a proposed 550-*megawatt* solar PV farm. It will cover nine square miles of desert near San Luis Obispo, and be the world's largest solar PV park when completed.

All the panels will be made by U.S.-based First Solar, the project owner, which now manufactures 1,000 megawatts of advanced solar PV capacity annually. This marks the entry of solar as a head-to-head competitor of U.S. utility-scale nuclear, coal and natural gas power plants. The First Solar project, and a different 250 Mw solar park, will deliver grid power at precisely the time California is most vulnerable to blackouts, and pre-empt higher peak price payments.

150

But this is not a one-off success. There are already solar competitors racing to win utility contracts and market share away from First Solar with different technologies in different U.S. states. They range in size from 5 to 500 megawatts. Many use solar PV arrays which feature diverse materials that trade off efficiency and production cost. Some use layered combinations of exotic elements to improve output. Some use hundreds of acres of panels or parabolic mirrors to collect the sunshine, then transfer the concentrated heat to conventional turbines and generators. Some use panels at a fixed angle, while others use more expensive tracking devices to maximize solar collection.

But there is no doubt that solar technologies now reliably perform at outputs from 5 kilowatts to 500 megawatts. They can supply many of the 600,000 villages in India, a remote village in the Amazon, Calcutta or a city in California. The factories to produce these solar technologies can and are being located in China, India, California, Taiwan and Portugal.

And there are promising signs that the next generation of solar PV panels will soon be more efficient and less expensive. Spectrolab, a research arm of the U.S. aerospace giant Boeing, announced in late 2006 that under laboratory conditions it had achieved a 40% efficiency in converting sunlight into power in a solar cell using new semi-conductor materials. This effectively doubles the current generation efficiency. The Spectrolab results were confirmed by an independent laboratory.[196]

Then in May, 2008, IBM Research declared a breakthrough in solar research which may lead to a five-fold increase in the efficiency of solar concentrating technology, and related major reductions in component costs. It uses exotic metals to extract heat and keep the solar cells cooler and more efficient.[197] That was followed by successful tests at the Massachusetts Institute of Technology in late 2008 which indicated a doubling of solar PV efficiency could be achieved with diverse reflective and anti-reflective coatings, which could also dramatically slash the costs of the most expensive panel component, silicon.

There are also astonishing advances in solar production techniques, such as factory lines which continuously roll out micro-thin sheets of PV panel materials similar to the way newspaper is produced at paper mills, or 'print' pliable, multi-layered solar panel circuits with several exotic metals which

---

[196] Dana Childs, Cleantech report, December 7, 2006
[197] Renewable Energy World, May 28, 2008

each capture a different part of the light spectrum.[198] These and similar breakthroughs allow solar PV technology to be incorporated into office tower windows, building shells, roofing tiles, sun-exposed surfaces like transport truck or car roofs, even the textiles of awnings or tents.

But this is not even the best current news. Parallel advances in wind turbine technology, performance and price reductions during the past two decades have put it far out in front of solar as measured by aggregate global power output.

In 2008 alone, global installed wind capacity grew by 27,000 megawatts (twice the total existing nuclear capacity in Canada) and brought the world-wide installed total to 121,000 megawatts. Half the new wind capacity was built in the U.S. and China. The global wind industry now accounts for some 440,000 related jobs.[199]

New wind installations will likely accelerate in the coming decade, with the advent of larger and more efficient turbines, offshore projects, and policies which promote green technologies, cap carbon emissions, and put a price on carbon pollutants. The World Wind Energy Association predicts installed global wind capacity of 1,500,000 megawatts of capacity by 2020 - a twelve-fold increase above 2008.[200]

The current global surge in solar, wind and other renewable technologies like hydro, geothermal, and biomass power plants, however, represents only a mere fraction of what could be delivered globally under a revolutionary - and widely replicable - green stimulus model first pioneered and perfected by Germany.

Called a feed-in tariff and backed by federal legislation, it requires all electric utilities and transmission line operators in Germany to purchase and connect all green power which can be delivered at prices guaranteed under a 20-year contract. The prices are calculated to allow the producers to recover all capital and interest costs, plus a modest profit, over the contract period.

The prices vary by technology type, size and location, but are the same within each segment so that offshore wind farms all receive the same tariff, which is different from inland wind farms. Solar farms get one price, while

---

[198] For example, the Helio-Volt Corp. plant in Austin, Texas.
[199] World Wind Energy Report, 2008
[200] ibid, pg 9

those systems on commercial buildings, or residential rooftops, receive different prices. There is a different price for farm biogas, or small hydro.

The genius of this model is that it allows wide entry into the power production system and multiple project scales - but the public never bails out failures. Under the 'pay for performance' system, only power actually delivered gets paid for. If the project technology fails to work, or there are cost overruns, or bad management, the producer eats the loss. This applies to a large wind farm, or each of the 400,000 owners of German grid-connected rooftop solar systems.

The aggregate costs of this new green power are blended into all monthly customer bills, so that all German electricity users pay a small portion of the green power premium. In 2009, this amounted to an extra $50 per year per household, or about $4 extra per month.

The green dividends have been astonishing. Despite mediocre wind sources and solar gain levels comparable to Alaska, Germany has become a world leader in domestic renewable power production, technology development, green collar jobs, and export orders. Grid-connected green power production in Germany more than doubled between 2000 and 2007, and will double again by 2020. This surge in economic activity has created 250,000 jobs, and generates annual revenues of $40 billion.[201]

This elegantly simple mechanism has revolutionized the electric power business in Germany the way cell phones, laptop computers and the Internet have changed communications. Now, instead of eighty-three million people depending on a few dozen giant coal and nuclear 'mainframes' hard-wired to the grid and sending power one way, nearly half a million green German 'laptop' producers are generating local power from wind farms, solar parks, farm biogas digestors, small hydro plants, and residential rooftops.

All this has been accomplished without building any new nuclear plants, and while Germany's greenhouse gas emissions were simultaneously cut by 20%. And its green potential is far from tapped out. According to a 2009 report by the German renewable energy association, it fully expects green power to grow at a torrid pace of 9 per cent annually and supply 278 billion kilowatt-hours of green power in 2020, or nearly half of national electric demand.[202]

---

[201] "Feed-in Frenzy", Chris Turner, Walrus Magazine, December, 2008
[202] Bundesverband Erneurbare Energie, (BEE) January, 2009

153

German's feed-in tariff success has attracted international envy and the highest form of flattery - imitation - in France, Spain, Portugal, Greece, Ireland and even Ontario, Canada. It has ignited similar explosions of economic activity, employment, innovation and entrepreneurship everywhere it has been initiated.

Since it serves people and the planet well, and the 'solar constant' which ultimately drives all green technologies abounds everywhere on Earth, there is no reason Germany's brilliant idea cannot be replicated wherever there are electric grids in the U.S., India, Africa, South America, Australia, Russia and China.

If and when that happens, nuclear plants, uranium and the proliferation threats they innately bear can be consigned to footnotes of history.

COMMERCE WITH A CONSCIENCE

The law locks up the hapless felon
Who steals the goose from off the common
But lets the greater felon loose
Who steals the common from the goose.

Old English proverb

It is a fact that in the last half century, humankind has created the means to destroy itself and much of animate creation. We have invented atomic arms, and the methods to proliferate more. The unrestrained use of fossil fuels threatens climatic chaos.

That's all down to us. So is whether we choose an exit strategy.

It is also a fact that there *is* one - the 'solar constant' which blesses our planet each day disguised as mere benign sunshine. Although it appears to have no substance, it is as real as uranium, more abundant than all the fossil fuels ever burned, just as practical, and perfectly clean. It has a half-life of forever. It is *wealth*.

This is a conceptual challenge, perhaps because our senses tell us real, practical value takes shape as a solid - as land, wood, oil, uranium, coal, a house, a tool, gold bullion, or money. But by adjusting the focus to basic physics, we can convert the renewable wealth which flows from the 'solar constant' into an economic currency just like money, oil or uranium.

In a word, it is 'hydrogen'. Whether it is infused in solar energy constantly streaming from implosions 93 million miles away, or in our air and oceans, the most plentiful element in our universe can be measured like money, divided into units equivalent to cents, dimes and dollars, and spent, saved, or traded in human commerce.

In fact, since it is utterly reliant on the 'solar constant', all of biological nature currently operates as a dynamic hydrogen economy, and even hydrocarbons (fossil fuels) are a form of stored solar energy. When coal is burned in power plants, the hydrogen which is combusted we measure in kilowatts or megawatts. We count the hydrogen burned in oil by the barrel, gallon or litre, or in natural gas by the cubic foot.

155

The problem is not that humanity uses these - the problem is that we are plundering these hydrocarbons from the distant past and burning too much, too fast and too inefficiently, in the present. Only a fraction of the hydrogen embedded in these fossil fuels actually delivers energy value - and the accumulating waste carbon dioxide is dangerously de-stabilizing our climate. There is a smart way to use hydrocarbons.[203]

Uranium is different. As a matter of physics, it is a uniquely *un*stable exception among elements - a kind of menacing, neutron-emitting outlaw which threatens the integrity and equilibrium of the biological world.

Imprisoned underground, uranium is essentially harmless. But when it is mined and fissioned in a reactor, it transmutes into more than two hundred elements which emit their own deadly neutrons. Metaphorically, and as a fact of physics, the sole uranium outlaw creates a malevolent *gang* of radioactive elements.

One of those gangsters is plutonium. It takes only an 8-kilogram, plum-sized sphere to make an atomic bomb which can destroy a city. Currently, some 65 million kilograms of uranium are being fissioned every year in power reactors around the globe. Inside them, enough plutonium is accumulating to make 7,000 warheads annually.

The outlaw nature of uranium also tends to destabilize human character and commerce, and leave a trail of tragedy. It led to Albert Einstein's most profound personal regret, and left a deep stain on brilliant scientists like J. Robert Oppenheimer and Andrei Sakharov, designer of the Soviet H-bomb.

It has also tempted traitors like Klaus Fuchs, fostered criminal espionage from Lavrentii Beria to A.Q. Khan, and driven dictators like Stalin, Jorge Videla and Kim Jung II to acquire it at any cost. It compelled U.S. President Harry Truman to vapourize two Japanese civilian targets in 1945, then order the production of another 20,000 even more powerful bombs. It tempted Israel to build a clandestine bomb, and Shimon Peres into a secret atomic test pact with the odious apartheid regime of South Africa. And it

---

[203] The 2006 Stern Report advised that greenhouse gas concentrations in the atmosphere must not exceed 500 parts per million, and that this would require a 50 per cent reduction in global carbon equivalent emissions (calibrated to 2005 emission levels) by 2050. More recent data suggest the average concentrations must be lower than 500 ppm.

enticed Indira Gandhi to betray a Canadian aid program and ignite an atomic arms race in the Indian sub-continent.

It has also lured Canada into a commerce without conscience.

Our country currently accounts for one-third of world uranium production. The Saskatchewan mine owners, and politicians in Ottawa and Regina, would be delighted to increase that export volume, and use uranium as a sweetener for CANDU reactor sales as well. They are still leading "Team Canada" trade missions to India or China, and pinning a proud Canadian flag on $1 billion worth of uranium atoms as they are shipped out of the country.

Keeping a tradition going back to the 1950's, the prevailing attitude in Ottawa and Regina has been that since Saskatchewan's uranium exports are a good thing, by definition there can't be enough. Even when the destination was explicitly military, federal prime ministers such as Lester Pearson and John Diefenbaker gave private uranium mines political and price support, while soaring profits accrued to the federally-owned Eldorado Nuclear.

Since 1945, left-leaning or arch-conservative Saskatchewan premiers have all, without exception, endorsed 'peaceful' uranium exports - in part because provincial co-ownership or royalty revenues gave them a vested interest in being nuclear boosters. Even the patron saint of social democrats, Tommy Douglas, pressed Ottawa hard in the 1950's to bankroll Saskatchewan uranium mine development and support exports.

The tradition continues. In recent years, rival Saskatchewan premiers Lorne Calvert [204] and Brad Wall have endorsed selling uranium to customers as diverse as the U.S., France, South Korea and Communist China. In some cases, trips to Washington and Beijing were made to court buyers and make sales pitches in person. All safeguards obligations have been adroitly assigned to Ottawa, which adroitly assigns them to no one.

Proving that amnesia can trump history, in early 2009 Conservative federal trade minister Stockwell Day took a trade mission to India, where he offered uranium and CANDU reactors to the very nation which betrayed Canada by using a research reactor to produce plutonium for its first bomb in 1974. The same offer was simultaneously extended to Pakistan, despite

---

[204] The NDP premier met with U.S. vice-president Dick Cheney to promote Saskatchewan uranium and heavy-oil production and sales in February, 2006.

its nuclear weapons status. Both nations remain NPT *outlieres*, have refused to sign the comprehensive nuclear test ban treaty, and continue to make more nuclear weapons. In 2007, India tested an Agni III missile which could strike Beijing or Shanghai. Assisted by North Korea and China, Pakistan has developed missiles meant to strike Delhi.

With a working assumption that 'profitable' must be a synonym for 'peaceful', all this commerce is done with official assurances that nuclear safeguards can prevent illicit use of Canadian uranium. Yet Ottawa effectively gutted the core mission of the Non-Proliferation Treaty by agreeing in 2008 to resume nuclear trade with India, a non-NPT signatory, if it segregated some atomic facilities and fuels for IAEA inspections, leaving designated nuclear weapons production sites off-limits.[205]

Setting aside the fact that India had previously betrayed Ottawa on its 'peaceful use' vow, this sent a chilling message to other potential proliferators that the punishment for pursuing weapons would be *increased* civilian nuclear commerce with Canada. The Harper government's reversal of the long-standing ban on nuclear trade with India, which followed the reckless lead of former U.S. president George W. Bush, was condemned by many NPT member countries and proliferation experts.

The 'peaceful atom' might possibly be policeable if all fissile fuels and reactors were confined to strict international control, and a safeguards agency existed which had the money, marching orders, staff, rigorous audit practices, and authority to both prevent illicit nuclear use and punish proliferation outlaws.

But no such body exists, and the one which has that title, the IAEA, has served as a see-no-evil enabler in the horizontal spread of nuclear weaponry. North Korea, Iran and Libya (almost) are only the most recent examples of failure. But with the world inventory of plutonium in reactor spent fuel already at 1,740 tonnes, and its half-life of 240 centuries, there are epochs yet for more failures.

A world awash in fissile materials is precisely what physicists like Einstein and Oppenheimer feared, and the Smyth Report warned of, in the months following Hiroshima. Both scientists felt deep moral revulsion at the applied results of their brilliance - and knew this fateful invention could soon be replicated by far lesser minds.

---

[205] India proposed putting 15 of its 24 reactors under IAEA inspections, leaving the rest to produce enough fissile material for up to 50 additional warheads per year.

Einstein and Oppenheimer were dead right when they and many of their eminent colleagues, such as Nobel laureates Niels Bohr and James Franck,[206] warned that the only way to preclude this peril was to either quarantine all fissile materials under U.N. control, or forswear producing fissile elements by enforcing a U.N. prohibition on uranium mining - the source of all U_{235} and Pu_{239}.

Given this, it seems evident that if they were alive today, they would argue that is pathological to keep shipping more and more Canadian uranium to foreign ports as if there is no catastrophic risk ahead, and it is merely another commodity like wood, wheat, or tempered steel.

But as John F. Kennedy warned in 1961, uranium and its latent capacity to destroy will physically and psychologically *enslave* the future. It is time to heed these wise scientific voices, and Kennedy's metaphor, and abolish a form of commerce as sinister as 18th century cargoes of chained African bodies.

There is a way to wind down the world-wide trade in uranium and power reactors, with relatively little pain, by recycling the basic bargain of the "Atoms for Peace" accord.

As adopted by the U.N. in 1956, and enshrined in the IAEA and Non-Proliferation Treaty, the *quid pro quo* was that most countries would forswear nuclear weapons if they were compensated with civilian nuclear fuels, technology and technical training. The existing weapons states also agreed to help finance this, and dismantle their atomic weapons.

It was a very bad bargain. Today there are 27,000 nuclear weapons aimed at human populations, a growing crowd of nuclear-armed nations, and the new threat of dirty 'backpack' bombs covertly acquired by terrorists or sub-national groups from ever-increasing stockpiles of plutonium.

But the basic deal can be salvaged by scrapping the fatal assumption that the *quid pro quo* must be more civilian atoms for less military ones. If the

---

[206] This warning was contained in a report James Franck drafted on behalf of many Manhattan Project scientists. It was intercepted by atomic bomb project commander Leslie Groves and never reached President Henry Truman.

U.N. member countries revise the mission so that 'energy solutions' replaces 'civilian atoms', then efficiency and renewables become the explicit reward for states which forswear all nuclear weaponry or commerce (excepting medical isotopes).

This would work as originally intended. The weapons states would commit to timelines and targets for eliminating nuclear weapons, and pay extra levies to the U.N. or allocate bi-lateral aid to fund efficiency and green power investments in non-weapons countries. Only countries which renounced *both* - and fulfilled formal accords to wind down their civilian nuclear programs or uranium production - would qualify for the assistance.

For example, the U.N. could promise North Korea funding to replace its entire electric power system with a no-cost package of renewable projects, efficiency investments, industrial cogeneration[207] and smart grid technologies. This would give it a modern, low-cost platform for economic development. In return, North Korea would permanently dismantle all its atomic facilities, military and civilian.

This would undoubtedly cost tens of billions. But the alternative is far worse. A nuclear-tipped long-range Nadong missile might suddenly strike Tokyo or Hawaii. Also, Japan and South Korea already have enough civil reactor plutonium, and the technical expertise, to build their own fission weapons within two years.

It could also be argued that North Korea should not receive billions in beneficial energy aid to dismantle dangerous nuclear facilities. Yet a dozen G8 countries, including Canada, are currently sharing in the $20 billion cost to dismantle warheads and fissile stockpiles inside Russia and former Soviet Union states. Canada has pledged $1 billion over ten years to secure and destroy this plutonium and enriched uranium.

Few would argue this is not a wise investment. Why not craft pre-emptive aid policies for countries like North Korea and Iran which solve both world security and energy problems with the same dollars?

The U.N. assistance could be delivered through the nascent International Renewable Energy Agency (IRENA), a multi-lateral effort launched by Germany, Spain and Denmark in January, 2009 to foster global renewable

---

[207] Also known as combined heat and power, this class of technologies converts currently wasted industrial and commerical heat into electric power. This doubles efficiency, and provides two energy products instead of one.

160

development. Using initial funds pledged by G8 countries, IRENA could provide qualifying member countries with technical assistance, and fund actual efficiency or renewable projects to those nations most in need, through a dedicated capital pool largely sustained by funding from G8 weapons states until they eliminate their own arsenals.

Like the "Atoms for Peace" plan, this would assist the poorest countries by providing them the most funds on a per capita basis, the fastest, for state-of-the-art green projects and related capacity building. The money would be conditional on retiring nuclear facilities, sound business plans, meeting construction milestones, operational performance, and audits to prevent or expose potential corruption. This would help solve energy and poverty problems, gradually reduce and end global nuclear commerce, and eliminate the 'civilian' camouflage which masks atomic proliferation.

There would be a higher proportional expense for the weapons states, but their levies would fall as they reduced their atomic arsenals, and those levies would be offset by reduced military spending as the threat of atomic attack recedes. The annual levies paid to IRENA via the U.N. could be considered premiums paid for anti-proliferation insurance. The toughest task would be how to treat major uranium producing countries like Canada, Australia, South Africa and Namibia. This kind of U.N. plan would cause the price of uranium to plummet, the producing companies would be left with worthless assets, and governments like the province of Saskatchewan would lose royalty payments and taxes.

Like any company selling an unsafe product from tobacco to asbestos to ozone-destroying chemicals, it could be argued they deserve a fatal loss of sales and market share because their product is deadly. But that would likely subvert any prompt U.N. adoption, because uranium producers like Cameco, and governments like those in Regina and Ottawa, would inevitably debate and diplomatically delay an outright ban for decades.

History has confirmed these same Canadian companies and governments have been prepared to join an illegal cartel to protect the uranium industry, sell it to despots and dictators, and continue to pretend the peaceful atom has no military alter ego. They have their counterparts in Australia, South Africa, Niger, Namibia and Kazakhstan.

A more effective way might be to impose a total global ban on new uranium production by 2012, using the successful Montreal Protocol model used for eliminating ozone-depleting substances. This would allow uranium companies like Cameco or Areva to supply current customers at existing contract prices, but not open any new mines (including Cigar Lake) as of 2012.

Given the current uranium production levels, and stalled nuclear reactor orders in the U.S. and Europe, this would cause a crash in uranium prices and make all new uranium mine development economically unviable. With no new uranium mines as of 2012, the 'choke point' for proliferation would relentlessly contract, then eventually seal off additional world supplies of fissile material. Verifying permanent bans on uranium mining could easily be done by satellites.

The winding down of uranium mining would effectively end potential new reactor sales from countries like Canada, France and the U.S. But the development and sales efforts by AECL have always been heavily subsidized. In fact, they have tripled since the Stephen Harper government was elected in 2006, during which it devoted $1.7 billion in nuclear subsidies. The 2008-09 federal fiscal budget allocated $658 million, and $574 million for the following year [208]

Ending these subsidies will actually be a major savings for federal taxpayers. A senior advisor to Stephen Harper admitted in June, 2009, that after $30 billion in historic subsidies AECL remained a dysfunctional 'sinkhole' in need of major restructuring and a private sector partner with deep pockets.[209]

Acting on an independent report, the Harper government put AECL on the sales block and vowed to resist building a replacement for the shutdown-prone 52-year old NRU reactor at Chalk River. The production of medical isotopes can be done in existing small research reactors in several countries under U.N. auspices. Once the isotopes are extracted, the small amounts of spent fuel can be isolated and eventually buried along with the waste from dismantled nuclear weapons production plants. These wastes are not a proliferation risk. A safer alternative technology – particle accelerators – can produce medical isotopes without creating lethal wastes.

Phasing out uranium exports would fortify and quicken the pace of current efforts to reduce world nuclear weapon arsenals. From a peak of 65,000 warheads in the early 1980's, the total world has fallen to 27,000. Of that total, the U.S. accounts for nearly 10,000, Russia 16,000, and the remaining

---

[208] Canadian Press, Bruce Cheadle, March 10, 2009
[209] "Tories Call AECL $30 Billion Sinkhole"; Canadian Press, June 12, 2009

weapons states of China, Britain, France, Israel, India, Pakistan and North Korea account for the balance.[210]

The United States and Russia have also committed to further reductions in operationally deployed strategic nuclear weapons by 2012, and a protocol under which both nations verifiably destroy the U_{235} and Pu_{239} in retired warheads and reduce their fissile material stockpile.[211] This includes 600 tonnes in Russia and former Soviet Union states. One of them, the Ukraine, voluntarily ceded control of the world's third largest nuclear weapons arsenal when it became independent.

These inspiring efforts have been augmented by multi-lateral commitments to dramatically reduce long-range missiles, prohibit new nuclear weapons testing, and agreements to jointly eliminate chemical and biological weapons of mass destruction. This success has taken decades of patient diplomacy, and billions in funding.

But the biggest threat of sabotaging this hard-won increase in world security comes from escalating uranium exports. At precisely the time Canada is assisting in a G8 program to destroy 34 tonnes of Russian Cold War plutonium,[212] and international protocols to prevent the spread of weapons of mass destruction are strengthening, Canada is recklessly flooding world markets with uranium which will be fissioned into far more plutonium than that destroyed.[213]

It is like a pyromaniac dressed as a fire-fighter surreptitiously adding gasoline to a dwindling but still dangerous wild fire.

Fortuitously, no additional global nuclear commerce is necessary. Increasingly intelligent energy efficiency practices, and the global advent of renewables, have made uranium and reactors irrelevant. These are also uneconomic, and a remedy for greenhouse gas emissions which will also kill

---

[210] "Bomb Scare"; Cirincione, pg 42
[211] G8 Global Partnership Against the Spread of Weapons and Materials of Mass Destruction
[212] This is enough plutonium for 6,000 warheads. The U.S. has also accepted 500 tonnes of highly enriched uranium from Russian warheads (and those of former Soviet states) for dilution and burning in civilian reactors.
[213] The G8 entity is the Multilateral Plutonium Disposition Group.

the patient. Worst of all, the wastes they create will present a security threat for hundreds of centuries.

By contrast, an intrinsic value of renewable energy technologies is that they can produce power and reduce greenhouse gases without creating collateral damage like radioactive wastes. Until recently, this advantage was offset by higher costs, and uncertain performance. However, that threshold has now been crossed. The proof is that by every important measure - global growth in component production and installed capacity, increasing performance-cost ratios, market share, new orders - renewables are on a remarkable ascent.

This will accelerate with the inevitable increase in oil and natural gas prices due to resource depletion rates and higher extraction costs. Also, the imminent imposition of carbon taxing or cap-and-trade systems to reduce greenhouse gas emissions, such as that now deployed in Europe, and the one proposed for North America by the Obama administration, will make all fossil fuels, including coal, much more expensive.

As these become more costly, efficiency and renewable investments will become increasingly attractive for purely economic reasons. In the electricity sector, the level of efficiency and renewable investments will be benchmarked to the future "avoided cost" of a major rival, nuclear. As now occurs in California, utilities will select the portfolio of options which deliver either energy reductions, or renewable supply, at a cost cheaper than or equal to the projected costs of new nuclear output.

This kind of comparison shopping, known as least cost planning, long ago brought new reactor orders in the United States to a halt. Not a single new firm order has been placed since 1978, and the latest cost calculations show that new nuclear plants have no future in the world's largest economy.

An incisive 2008 analysis by American certified public accountant Craig Severence predicts that new nuclear plant expenses (construction capital, interest, fuel, operations) will mean typical production costs of $.25 to $.30 per kilowatt-hour.[214] This is *triple* the price new windfarms are charging to electric utilities after competitive bidding in the U.S. and Canada,[215] and less than the delivered cost of large solar PV projects such as those contracted for in California and Arizona.

---

[214] "Business Risks and Costs of Nuclear Power"; Craig Severence, CPA,
[215] Winning wind farm bids for a 2007 renewable energy RFP by the Ontario Power Authority averaged 8.8 cents/kwhr.

These fatal nuclear reactor construction costs will directly affect sales of Canadian uranium. If there are no future reactor orders from the United States, which now accounts for eighty per cent of world demand, the global uranium market will eventually drop by 54 million pounds annually.[216]

Nuclear power has been aptly described as "a future technology whose time has already passed". But we need not lament its demise, because the 'solar constant' and hydrogen economy beckons.

We can already discern its outlines. Giant wind turbines patiently spin in Copenhagen's harbour, or silently harvest desert winds near Aswan, Egypt. Huge solar arrays grace parched slopes in Spain, or silently track the sun with parabolic mirrors near Phoenix, Arizona. Hydro-electric plants from Niagara Falls to Norway use mere gravity and water flows driven by the sun to create clean power. Some 30 million solar hot water heaters begin work every morning in China when the sun comes up. Cellulostic enzymes are being deployed to convert grasses, crop residues and forest wastes into biofuel. Pilot projects now produce power from the tides, waves, and ocean algae biomass. Geothermal plants compliment hydro sites in Iceland.

But even better prospects lie just ahead. At the right scale, several renewable technologies have the ability to split atoms and make hydrogen itself. This can be achieved by sending an electric current through ordinary water, which causes the hydrogen and oxygen atoms to separate. The hydrogen can be collected as a gas, then stored like lightning in a bottle.

This can radically redefine the global energy future. Unlike electricity, hydrogen gas is an energy 'currency' which can be banked in fuel cells or bottled, then spent in infinite ways, in infinite locations. It can pump well water, light a school, run power tools, fuel a cargo ship, airplane, city bus, transport truck or passenger car, heat a home, air condition a hospital or shopping mall, or drive industrial machinery.

This is not science fiction. Hydrogen was first distilled on an industrial scale a century ago, using the electricity from a hydro plant in Norway to split

---

[216] The amount of uranium imported into the U.S. in 2007.

water molecules. But the same "electrolysis" process can be renewably powered by large scale wind farms, solar parks, geothermal plants, or biogas digestors. There is an efficiency penalty when electricity is converted to hydrogen, but being able to bottle energy and use it precisely when and where it is needed can be more valuable.

Currently, an electric utility in Spain is using Canadian fuel cell technology to convert off peak wind power into hydrogen, which can then be re-converted back into electricity and seamlessly supply the grid exactly when demand is highest. The only emissions are ordinary water. This transforms intermittent wind power into just-in-time delivered energy, and avoids the need to build another power plant to supply that power. The Canadian company, Hydrogenics Corp., has a similar wind farm/hydrogen fuel cell project in Chile, and a pilot project with a wind farm on Prince Edward Island.

The same electrolysis/hydrogen hybrid technology can be matched with large solar farms in the Sahara, the Rajasthan region in northern India, the Gobi Desert in China, outback Australia, or Mexico's Sonoma desert. The bulk hydrogen could be sent into electric grids to match demand, delivered to cities in a pipeline, trucked like gasoline to supply mobile fuel depots, or shipped across oceans to supply island nations like Great Britain, Japan, New Zealand or Madagascar.

In fact, Iceland has adopted an official national plan to become a self-sufficient, zero-carbon society by producing all its energy from hydro-electric sites and geothermal steam escaping to the surface from the earth's core. The latter can be captured and used to drive turbines and generators.

The two Icelandic energy 'currencies' will be electricity and hydrogen. The grid will be used to deliver electrons for lights, computers, motors, power tools, and industrial machinery, while the hydrogen will be used principally for buses, vehicles, Iceland's fleet of fishing boats, space and water heating, and some commercial processes.

This plan for the world's first hydrogen economy is under full construction now. Iceland's geothermal sites have been mapped, and some of the projects are already operating. Gas stations and public transit buses are being converted to use hydrogen. Nearly ninety per cent of Iceland's economy already runs on renewables - and the last ten per cent will almost certainly be erased in less time and cost than it would take to order, approve and build new nuclear plants.

166

There is no reason Iceland's renewable/hydrogen hybrid technology cannot be replicated in the rest of the world, using different mixes of renewable resources. This can be the decisive technical means to increase global energy supplies while dramatically reducing greenhouse gases from fossil fuel combustion. Unlike nuclear plants, the only waste this will produce is harmless water.

But the hydrogen economy also holds the potential to re-distribute world wealth, and reduce global poverty and geo-political conflicts. Sophisticated new satellite mapping technologies, which can accurately predict potential solar and wind power output per square meter from the stratosphere, now confirm that most of the globe's richest renewable assets are in the very regions where poverty is highest.

The biggest potential is from solar-derived hydrogen produced in equatorial and sub-tropic deserts and highly-arid regions, and from wind farms along the ocean coasts of South America, Africa, India and China. A key feature of this potential is that sunshine and wind, unlike an oil reserve, diamond deposit, or platinum mine, represent a form of potential wealth which is intrinsically resistant to monopolization and corruption.

This is because renewable technologies, and even hydrogen electrolysis, can often be scaled up from the community level to the large industrial complex. A 10-kilowatt rooftop solar photo-voltaic array on a southern Africa school or health clinic, or a wind turbine, can provide electricity to a bank of batteries, or be used to create small amounts of hydrogen for cooking, a portable generator, or small scooter.

Industrial-scale hydrogen production from solar or wind *will* require large amounts of capital. This would tend to keep the ownership of production plants and related renewable resources in effective control of the few in poor nations that already have considerable investment capital.

But if, as proposed in the previous chapter, some of these renewable and hybrid hydrogen projects are largely financed through a revised United Nations "atoms for peace" mechanism to reward nations which forswear or renounce nuclear power development, a condition of IRENA and U.N. financing could be that they are built as public infrastructure projects under the auspices of a utility, development corporation, municipal government, or co-operative. This would ensure a greater public share in the benefits.

This would not preclude private investors from constructing similar for-profit projects which are ineligible for U.N. funding, or submitting competitive tender bids to supply equipment, components or services for the IRENA funded projects. One need not assume that only capitalism, or non-profit social entrepreneurship, are exclusively capable of success. Given the abundance of undeveloped renewable resources, there is enough wealth, and work, for both forms of commerce.

This clarifies an ethical choice for Canada and its role in the community of nations.

A doubling of global nuclear power will require some 450 more large reactors. They will be costly, deliver uncertain performance, rely on finite uranium deposits, operate at best for several decades, fail to serve most poor rural populations, produce long-lived radioactive wastes, and create enough plutonium for several hundred thousand nuclear warheads. This would deliver only an extra five per cent of world energy production.

By contrast, a diverse array of renewable and hybrid-hydrogen technologies can underpin the construction of an unlimited number of new power plants world-wide, using free fuel, at less cost, with better performance, and serve the poorest populations best while reducing greenhouse gases in every energy sector and producing only ordinary water as waste.

Although it profits some, uranium and reactor exports embed innate risks, including radioactive wastes and plutonium which will imperil collective security for hundreds of centuries. That is a fact of physics.

But a far better choice beckons, because physics also tells us that the miraculous 'solar constant' which blesses our planet can underwrite an infinitely abundant, technically elegant and egalitarian hydrogen economy which can deliver pollution-free energy, prosperity and peace.

This windfall awaits.

168

SELECTED SOURCES

Bernstein, Jeremy; *Plutonium: A History of the World's Most Dangerous Element*; Joseph Henry Press; 2007

Bothwell, Robert; *Eldorado: Canada's National Uranium Company*; University of Toronto Press; 1984

Bothwell, Robert; *Nucleus: The History of Atomic Energy of Canada Limited*; University of Toronto Press; 1988

Buckley, Brian; *Canada's Early Nuclear Policy: Fate, Chance and Character*; McGill-Queen's University Press; 2000

Cathcart, Brian; *The Fly in the Cathedral*; Penguin; 2004

Chang, Gordon; *Nuclear Showdown*; Random House; 2006

Cirincione, Joseph; *Bomb Scare: The History and Future of Nuclear Weapons*; Columbia University Press; 2007

Eggleston, Wilfred; *Canada's Nuclear Story*; Clarke Irwin; 1965

Finch, Ron; *Exporting Danger*; Black Rose; 1986

Goodchild, Peter; *Oppenheimer: The Father of the Bomb*; Ariel; 1980

Gyorgy, Anna; *No Nukes; Everyone's Guide to Nuclear Power*; Black Rose Books; 1979

Harding, Jim; *Canada's Deadly Secret: Saskatchewan Uranium and the Global Nuclear System*; Fernwood; 2007

Hersh, Seymour; *The Samson Option*; Random House; 1991

Holloway, David; *Stalin and the Bomb*; Yale University Press; 1984

Hyde, Montgomery; *The Atom Bomb Spies*; Hamish Hamilton; 1980

Karpin, Michael; *The Bomb in the Basement*; Simon and Schuster; 2006

Knight, Amy; *Beria: Stalin's First Lieutenant*; Princeton University Press; 1993

Knight, Amy; *How The Cold War Began*; McClelland and Stewart;

Langewiesche, William; *The Atomic Bazaar*; Farrar, Strauss, Giroux; 2007

Lovins, Amory; *Energy/War: Breaking the Nuclear Link*; Friends of the Earth; 1980

Lovins, Amory; *Soft Energy Paths*; Harper & Row; 1977

McKay, Paul; *The Roman Empire*; Key Porter; 1990

McPhee, John; *The Curve of Binding Energy*; Ballantine Books; 1973

Patterson, Walter; *The Plutonium Business*; Paladin Books; 1984

Percovitch, George; *India's Nuclear Bomb*; University of California Press; 1999

Pringle, Peter and Spigelman, James; *The Nuclear Barons*; Holt, Rinehart, Winston; 1981

Regehr, Ernie and Rosenblum, Simon; *Canada and the Nuclear Arms Race*; James Lorimer; 1983

Schell, Jonathan; *The Seventh Decade*; Metropolitan; 2007

Sherwin, Martin; *A World Destroyed*; Vintage; 1973
Spector, Leonard; *The New Nuclear Nations*; Vintage Books; 1985
Timmerman, Kenneth; *Countdown to Crisis*; Crown Forum; 2005
Weissman, Steve and Krosney, Herbert; *The Islamic Bomb*; Times Books; 1981

A

A.Q. Khan, 85, 86, 88, 96, 102, 103, 104, 118, 119, 120, 121, 122, 123, 156
Acheson, Dean, 48, 112, 113
Acheson-Lillienthal Report, 48
AECL, 17, 68, 90, 91, 92, 93, 94, 95, 96, 97, 98, 99, 100, 101, 102, 128, 162
Ahmad, Ishfaq, 85, 86, 88
Ahmadinejad, Mahmoud, 125
Algoma, 61, 63
Areva, 24, 71, 104, 105, 106, 107, 109, 134, 161
Argentina, 16, 22, 89, 90, 91, 92, 94, 98, 119, 127
Athabasca, 70, 104, 105
Atlee, Clement, 43, 44
Atoms for Peace, 49, 76, 110, 111, 112, 114, 127, 159, 161
Australia, 21, 56, 63, 68, 104, 107, 154, 161, 166

B

Baruch, Bernard, 113, 114
BBC China, 103
Beaverlodge, 63, 64, 104
Beijiing, 4, 11
Ben-Gurion, David, 72, 73, 74
Bergmann, Ernst, 72, 73, 74
Beria, Laventrii, 9, 27, 38, 39, 42, 43, 44, 45, 50, 51, 52, 53, 54, 56, 135, 156, 169
Berlin, 27, 29, 61
Bhabha, Homi, 76, 77, 78, 79, 80, 81, 83, 114
Bhutto, Ali 10, 22, 81, 85, 87, 88, 120
Bikini atoll, 54, 113
biofuel, 146, 165
biogas, 153, 166
Bohr, Niels, 27, 29, 41, 55, 159
Brasil, 142, 143
breeder reactor, 77, 78, 79, 80, 133, 134, 135, 137

Britain, 7, 9, 16, 20, 23, 27, 28, 30, 31, 32, 35, 38, 44, 45, 49, 56, 62, 63, 66, 71, 72, 73, 83, 89, 96, 112, 114, 163, 166
Bushehr, 122, 123, 124
Byrnes, James, 113

C

California, 27, 130, 131, 148, 149, 150, 151, 164, 169
Calvert, Lorne, 157
Cambridge University, 25, 76
Cameco, 103, 104, 105, 106, 107, 109, 138, 161
CANDU, 8, 10, 11, 16, 21, 22, 23, 24, 35, 37, 47, 67, 68, 78, 79, 81, 82, 83, 84, 85, 86, 89, 90, 91, 92, 93, 94, 95, 96, 97, 98, 99, 100, 101, 102, 103, 107, 112, 116, 120, 126, 133, 135, 136, 143, 145, 157
Cap la Hague, 134
cartel, 21, 68, 69, 104, 105, 106, 161
Carter,Jimmy , 87, 92, 118
Cavendish Labratory, 77
CEA, 70, 71, 72, 73, 87
Ceausescu,Nicholi, 94, 95
Cernovada, 95
Chadwick, 25, 33, 51, 76
Chalk River, 7, 23, 36, 37, 38, 41, 47, 53, 56, 60, 63, 64, 71, 75, 76, 77, 78, 83, 114, 130, 162
Chashma, 87, 88
Cheliabinsk-40, 53, 135
Chernobyl, 135
Chicago, 31, 32, 36, 37, 38, 46, 55, 92, 130
China, 7, 11, 16, 20, 22, 23, 80, 82, 88, 91, 96, 97, 98, 99, 100, 101, 102, 103, 107, 112, 115, 116, 118, 119, 120, 121, 122, 123, 125, 129, 144, 146, 147, 151, 152, 154, 157, 158, 163, 165, 166, 167
Chretien, Jean, 15, 96, 97, 98, 99, 100, 101
Chun Doo Hwan, 93

171

172

H

Halban, Hans, 29, 30, 33, 34, 35, 36, 38
Halperin, Israel, 47
Hanford, 34, 131, 134
Harper, Stephen, 17, 103, 136, 158, 162, 169
Harwell, 37, 38, 45
H-bomb, 19, 23, 45, 46, 55, 62, 63, 67, 102, 156
heavy water, 19, 23, 29, 30, 31, 32, 33, 34, 35, 36, 41, 51, 52, 53, 54, 64, 71, 74, 78, 80, 82, 83, 87, 88, 102, 119, 120, 131
Hiroshima, 2, 5, 15, 19, 20, 25, 32, 38, 43, 45, 47, 49, 51, 55, 59, 60, 62, 76, 81, 109, 112, 141, 158
Hoover, Herbert 42, 44
House of Commons, 46, 63, 66
Howe, C.D., 59, 61, 65
hydrogen bomb, 6, 15, 20, 22, 25, 37, 44, 54, 62, 64, 65, 69, 71, 74, 80, 82, 96, 111, 119, 125, 135
Hydrogenics Corp., 166

I

IAEA, 86, 88, 94, 112, 114, 115, 116, 117, 118, 119, 120, 121, 122, 123, 124, 125, 126, 127, 128, 158, 159
IBM Research, 151
Iceland, 165, 166, 167
India, 7, 10, 16, 21, 22, 23, 72, 73, 74, 75, 76, 77, 78, 79, 80, 81, 82, 83, 84, 85, 87, 89, 90, 93, 101, 103, 107, 112, 114, 116, 119, 120, 121, 126, 127, 128, 129, 133, 134, 135, 142, 143, 144, 145, 146, 151, 154, 157, 158, 163, 166, 167, 169
International Atomic Energy Agency, 86, 112, 115, 130, 138
Iran, 7, 19, 75, 84, 88, 102, 103, 116, 119, 121, 122, 123, 124, 125, 126, 127, 129, 130, 135, 137, 158, 160
Iraq, 75, 87, 116, 119, 122, 127
IRENA, 160, 161, 167, 168
Isfahan, A. 122

Israel, 7, 16, 23, 33, 47, 72, 73, 74, 75, 87, 112, 120, 122, 123, 124, 156, 163

J

Japan, 19, 26, 32, 47, 50, 51, 55, 68, 83, 88, 115, 133, 146, 160, 166
Jericho missile, 75, 122
Johnson, Lyndon 67
Joliot-Curie, Frederic, 26, 29, 33, 35

K

Kahuta, 88, 120
KANUPP, 84, 86, 87, 88
Kazakhstan, 54, 107, 161
Kennedy, John 15, 79, 159
Key Lake, 70, 105, 106, 108
Khariton, 51, 52, 54
Khushab, 88
Kiggavik, 107
Kim Jong Il, 115, 116, 118
King, Mackenzie, 15, 33, 39, 40, 41, 42, 43, 44, 46, 47, 60, 61
Kota, 79
Kowarski, Lew, 29, 30, 34, 36, 70, 71
Kurchatov, 51, 52, 53, 54

L

Lewis, W.B., 77, 78
Li Peng, 11, 96, 102, 103, 119, 123
Liberal, 11, 21, 61, 63, 64, 65, 66, 83, 84, 96, 97, 99, 103
Libya, 84, 88, 102, 103, 116, 119, 120, 121, 122, 126, 127, 158
lithium, 25, 45, 46, 62, 64, 80, 82, 102, 119
loan guarantee, 99, 102
London, 31, 33, 39, 41, 42, 43, 44, 48, 55, 61, 80, 121
London Club, 121
Lop Nor, 80, 116
Los Alamos, 31, 32, 33, 36, 38, 43, 44, 45, 62
Lovins, Amory 87, 88, 145, 147, 169

174